LETTING GO OF
SELF-DESTRUCTIVE BEHAVIORS

Letting Go of Self-Destructive Behaviors offers inspiring, hopeful, creative resources for the millions of male and female adolescents and adults who struggle with eating disorders, addictions, or any form of self-mutilation. It is also a workbook for the clinicians who treat them. Using journaling exercises, drawing and collaging prompts, guided imagery, visualizations, and other behavioral techniques, readers will learn how to understand, compassionately work with, and heal from their behaviors rather than distracting from or fighting against them, which can dramatically reduce internal conflict and instill genuine hope. Techniques are provided in easy-to-follow exercises that focus on calming the body, containing overwhelming emotions, managing negative and distorted thoughts, re-grounding from flashbacks, addressing tension and anxiety, decreasing a sense of vulnerability, strengthening assertiveness and communication skills, and accessing inner wisdom.

This workbook can be used in conjunction with *Treating Self-Destructive Behaviors in Trauma Survivors, Second Edition*, also by Lisa Ferentz, to allow therapists and their clients to approach the behaviors from the same strengths-based perspective. Workbook exercises can be completed as homework assignments or as part of a therapy session. In either case, the client is given the opportunity to process their work and share their insights with a compassionate witness and trained professional, making the healing journey even safer and more rewarding.

Lisa Ferentz, LCSW-C, is the president and founder of the Institute for Advanced Psychotherapy Training and Education, which provides continuing education to mental health professionals. She was named "Social Worker of the Year" by the Maryland Society for Clinical Social Work in 2009 and has been in solo private practice specializing in trauma for 30 years.

LETTING GO OF SELF-DESTRUCTIVE BEHAVIORS

A Workbook of Hope and Healing

Lisa Ferentz

Routledge
Taylor & Francis Group

NEW YORK AND LONDON

First published 2015
by Routledge
605 Third Avenue, New York, NY 10017
2 Park Square, Milton Park, Abingdon, Oxon OX14 4RN

Routledge is an imprint of the Taylor & Francis Group, an informa business

Images on pp. 3, 8, 11, 24, 33, 45, 53, 59, 65, 91, 96, 101, 108, 112, 118, 123, 127, 131, 137, 140, 147, 161, 190, 203, 217, 226, 243, 258, and 265 used courtesy of Shutterstock®, http://www.shutterstock.com

Library of Congress Cataloging in Publication Data
Ferentz, Lisa
Letting go of self-destructive behaviors: a workbook of hope and healing/by Lisa Ferentz
pages cm
Includes index
Letting Go of Self-Destructive Behaviors
Summary: Letting Go of Self-Destructive Behaviors offers inspiring, hopeful, creative resources for the millions of male and female adolescents and adults who struggle with eating disorders, addictions, and any form of self-mutilation. It is also a workbook for the clinicians who treat them"—Provided by publisher.
1. Self-destructive behavior—Treatment, 2. Self-destructive behavior in adolescence—Treatment.
3. Self-help techniques. I. Title.
RC569.5.S45F46 2015
616.85′82—dc23
2014011470

ISBN: 978-1-138-80076-2 (hbk)
ISBN: 978-1-138-80077-9 (pbk)
ISBN: 978-1-315-75528-1 (ebk)

Typeset in New Baskerville and Stone Sans
by Swales & Willis Ltd, Exeter, Devon, UK

For my beautiful grandmother, Fay Berkelhammer, 99 years young: Your love, wisdom, creativity, and extraordinary insights have been and will continue to be a source of inspiration and healing for generations to come.

For Kevin: We really are holding hands and reaching for the stars together.

And for all of my clients past and present: Thank you for teaching me, inspiring me, and always reminding me of the courage, creativity, and resiliency of the human spirit.

CONTENTS

FOREWORD

"Hurt people, hurt people." Most of us know this to be true. Unfortunately, hurt people very often hurt themselves. Many of these "hurt people" are ones who would never think of hurting another. However, they see nothing wrong with hurting themselves by cutting, burning themselves, drinking too much, eating too much, not eating, drugging, or doing other compulsive, addictive behaviors that are self-destructive. This book was written to help you understand the origins of your hurt and the *why* of your self-harming behavior.

One of the hardest things to do is to take that first step and admit that you need help. Then what? How do you find someone who can help you? Who do you call? What do you say? What questions do you even ask? After all, the therapist you are calling could be the one to help save your life! Finding someone to help is no easy task, especially when you may be depressed, scared, anxious, and feel you have nowhere to turn. Not to mention the shame you may be experiencing.

What you need to know, however, is that the therapist you choose must be trained in trauma therapy (emotional, physical, or sexual). Even if you think you grew up with the perfect family, somewhere you were hurt by someone who took your power away. It could have happened when you were a child, teenager, or even as an adult. Because you are hurting yourself, what you need most is the patience, care, and concern of a specially trained therapist who can help you understand the origins of your hurt and the reason for your self-harming behavior.

I'd like to explain a little of my story so that you can hear from a "real" person, who has "been there, done that." I was fortunate that I had a physician in whom I confided who gave me the name of a therapist. This was many years ago and self-harming behavior, especially cutting, was always looked at as a suicide attempt. Very long story short—I had childhood/teenage sexual abuse in my life as well as emotional neglect by my parents. I felt like I wanted to die. The only relief I could find was by hurting myself and drinking. Dissociation (zoning-out or going away in my head) was my way of life most days. I just figured I was crazy and wouldn't live very long. I was 38, had a great husband, two beautiful kids, a good job, nice house—but I wanted to die. Being crazy was my deepest, darkest secret. Finally, I had hit rock bottom and basically fell apart. Not only was I hurting myself but my actions were deeply hurting the people who loved me. I needed help.

I was very, very lucky. I found Lisa Ferentz, who was willing to listen to anything with care and concern and always with a helpful self-care suggestion rather than the usual, "how did that make you feel" or eyes that "glazed over" when told something "weird." You know what I mean!

Lisa didn't know a lot about dissociation or self-harming behavior back then. She tried to get me to do a contract not to hurt myself. Well, I thought that was just the dumbest thing anyone could ask me to do and I refused. After all, it was my body, and I was going to do what _I_ wanted to do to it. No one was EVER going to tell me what to do with it—my body was finally mine. If I wanted to hurt it, I would hurt it. To my surprise, she didn't fire me or threaten to hospitalize me. Instead, Lisa treated me with respect and we worked in collaboration to get to the root of the problem.

She took workshops, extra courses, read everything she could get her hands on about self-harming behavior and even contacted experts in the area of dissociation to get help. The point is, her mind was always open to new ideas and she was willing to work for me and with me. I always felt safe and able to confide anything, no matter how embarrassing, crazy, or weird I thought it was.

So how do you find someone with these qualities and who knows how to help? You need to ask the right questions when you make the call or calls to find a therapist. Get a few names from a doctor or recommendations from a friend who has been through therapy. You can easily search the Internet for someone near you. Type in _therapist-trauma-PTSD and the abbreviation for your state._ You should get the names of local therapists with information on their website about the types of therapy offered. Almost all therapists will talk to you for a few minutes free of charge and some have an e-mail address on their website for you to contact them.

It is imperative to find someone who is trained in _PTSD_ therapy (Post-traumatic Stress Disorder) and who works with _survivors of trauma._ These are the two most important "buzz" words to use when you call. If you can, tell them about hurting yourself and ask what they could do to help you. If you hear any negativity in their voice or the word "contract," politely thank them and hang up.

Back when I began my journey in therapy, it took much longer than it does today to end my cycle of self-harming behavior. But thanks to Lisa and her work in this field, many new techniques have been introduced to therapists to help clients, and they work! No contracts, no hospitals (unless you are suicidal) and techniques that NEVER take away your power. YOU are the one to decide how, why, and when to begin to take care of yourself in a positive, self-caring way.

Have faith that you will find someone to help you. In the meantime, this book can go a long way in getting you started on the path of self-care rather than self-harm. I wish there had been a workbook such as this when I was hurting myself. There wasn't much out there on the topic, and I know the more you can educate yourself the better off you'll be. This book is full of information for you in every area that you are dealing with such as how to cope with triggers, unpleasant scary feelings and most of all understanding the need to harm yourself. It will give you alternative ways to cope that will help you heal. In addition, this book is full of information on topics such as PTSD, abuse issues, dealing with others who don't understand what you are doing, and many, many more pieces of good advice.

Take it from me, I've been in your shoes. I couldn't imagine NOT hurting myself and thought Lisa was crazy to suggest I didn't have to! Now hurting myself is far from my mind and something I can't even imagine doing to myself. During my journey with Lisa I actually did most of the exercises in this book and I know they helped. In my opinion, Lisa's idea of using CARESS as a way to stop self-harming behavior is a breakthrough in trauma therapy.

Use this book at your own pace. It is best if you can use it with a therapist's help. But if you can't, at least you are taking a step in the right direction by arming yourself with knowledge and doing activities that will help you begin to cope in a healthy, powerful way. I will end by echoing Lisa's words, "You have what it takes to take care of yourself." And you do!

Good luck on your journey to wholeness and wellbeing. You can do it!

Margaret H. Grimes

ACKNOWLEDGMENTS

I am eternally grateful for the abundance of love, nurturance, and support I have received throughout my life from my wonderful parents, Burt and Sasha, and my extraordinary and accomplished siblings, Steven, Beth and David. I am able to pay it forward in the world because of your love and unwavering faith in me.

A heartfelt thank you and much love to all of my incredible friends, colleagues, Institute faculty, and Institute participants who so generously and graciously support my work. Special thanks to my cheerleaders, Denise Tordella, Robyn Brickel, Maria Hadjiyane, Trish Mullen, Sabrina N'Diaye, Dr. Patricia Papernow, Susan Osofsky, Nancy Napier, Debbie Marks, Peggy Kolodny, Susan Kachur, Amy Weintraub, and Joan Kristall. I am humbled by your enthusiasm and loving feedback, and I never take it for granted. Please know that I have the greatest respect for your contributions to the field.

Many thanks to my incredible assistants and partners in this journey: Gerri Baum, Kim Brandwin, and Renee Moore. Your energy, creativity, and willingness to always help have been a blessing in my life.

A heartfelt, special thank you to my editor and friend, Anna Moore, for your guidance and loving support, and for believing in my work. Thank you for always having my back and my best interests at heart. Thank you for helping me and empowering me to write the book I wanted to write.

I am also very grateful to the behind-the-scenes, talented people at Routledge and in the United Kingdom for your creative input and your endless patience. Thank you Elizabeth Graber, Julie Willis, Sarah Hudson, Julia Gardiner, Kate Reeves, and Paris West for being such great team players.

Thank you to Corinne Liccketto at Smith Publicity for your boundless enthusiasm and excitement about this project. I know with your guidance the work will reach so many people.

I continue to be indebted to the masterful researchers, clinicians, and authors in the trauma field for their work and their dedication to helping clients in their healing journeys. Thanks to Dusty Miller and Tracy Alderman for inspiring me with your groundbreaking work with self-destructive behaviors. I am especially grateful to Richard Schwartz for the many ways in which you have influenced my work with your brilliant Internal Family Systems model, and for your friendship and support.

An extra special thank you to Dr. Janina Fisher and Dr. Joyanna Silberg, dear friends, talented colleagues, and "co-mentors" for going above and beyond in your generous, insightful, and invaluable feedback and editing suggestions. You both helped to make this a better book.

I am forever grateful for the generosity and wisdom of Margaret Grimes. Your input and contributions to this book are beyond measure. Thank you for allowing me to sometimes be the student. Thank you for your willingness to pay it forward. You are a true inspiration.

Most importantly, thank you to my husband, soul mate, and editor extraordinaire, Kevin. Words cannot express how grateful I am for the countless ways in which you encourage, inspire, support, teach, nurture, and love me. You are my role model and daily reminder of the importance of making a difference in the world.

And to our three magnificent sons, Jacob, Zachary, and Noah, I love you with all of my heart and soul. It is a privilege, an honor, a delight, and a joy to be your Mom.

PART I

TAPPING INTO YOUR CURIOSITY AND COURAGE

1

BEGINNING THE JOURNEY

"I know that hurting my body isn't really a good idea, but I feel like I can't stop."

"When I starve all day, I feel kind of powerful. Until I feel dizzy and out of control again."

"When I hook up with men I don't know why my friends get upset. They seem a lot more worried about it than I do!"

"Drinking is a way to cope. Why can't my family understand that?"

"If I had another way to feel better and stop the pain inside of me, I guess I'd try, but I don't feel like there is any other way."

"At least when I'm thinking about my cutting, I'm not thinking about other things in my life that have hurt me!"

Do you relate to any of those thoughts? Do you ever feel scared or upset by your behaviors yet struggle with the idea of stopping or changing them? Have you ever tried to give them up but found it too hard? Having spent many years working with people who do self-destructive or self-harming behaviors, I've learned that the healing journey often begins with two main qualities: courage and curiosity. It takes tremendous courage to say, "There may be a problem with what I'm doing," or "It's possible that what I've been doing isn't working for me anymore." Being courageous doesn't mean that you're not afraid. In fact, if any of us waited until we weren't afraid before taking a challenging new step, we might never consider moving ahead. You can be afraid and do it anyway. Whether that means trying out a new behavior, entertaining a new idea, or letting go of old thoughts and behaviors that are familiar but are also harmful to your physical or emotional safety and wellbeing.

Once you notice your courage and tap into it, you can allow yourself to be curious about other options. This moves you even further along in your recovery process. Being curious about new possibilities works best when you approach this with an open heart and an open mind. It may feel natural for you to quickly judge or rule out new options. Change can feel scary, even when you're sure change will make things better for you. It's ok to be scared or confused as you consider new ways of coping. It's natural to hesitate when you don't have other ways of getting relief. Give yourself permission to be curious in a compassionate and non-judgmental way. In order to grow, you have to be curious – otherwise, things stay the same. They may be predictable but they aren't really better. You have already taken a step in the right direction by giving yourself permission to be curious about this workbook!

Although reading this and participating in the journaling, drawing, and behavior exercises can be an important step in helping you let go of your self-destructive behaviors, it's important to state that *no one can make you stop whatever it is you are doing*. The decision to be free of those behaviors and to replace them with healthier ones has to come from *you*. And the truth is it's really hard to give up what you *do* know—even if it seems to be creating problems for you—and replace it with behaviors you *don't* know—even if they appear to be in your best interest.

That's why the only thing you really need to get started is the willingness, the courage, to say, "Maybe there's a better way to get my needs met," and the curiosity to say, "I'm willing to listen and learn." In the end, the decision will be yours. The great news is there *are* other safer behaviors that allow you to achieve the temporary, positive results that you get from self-destructive behaviors. The difference is these new options will give you results that last, and won't create the same negative side effects that you are probably experiencing such as guilt, shame, fear, loss of control, or unwanted physical pain.

It's important to realize that there are positive benefits from your behaviors. You wouldn't be doing them if you didn't get something from them! It takes courage to admit that there are powerful negative outcomes as well. Together, we will explore the common positive and negative consequences of hurting the body or doing addictive behaviors. Understanding the "pay-off" can reduce the confusion and shame associated with why you keep going back to the behaviors. Understanding the very real downsides to your actions gives you the opportunity to re-think whether or not it would be in your best interest to learn other ways of coping and feeling better.

If you are like most people who abuse substances, have an eating disorder, engage in other addictive behaviors, or injure your body through acts of self-harm or self-mutilation, you have spent a lot of energy trying to explain the importance of your behaviors to loved ones, or attempting to downplay the negative consequences of your actions. This makes sense when those behaviors feel like the only helpful way to soothe or be numb, distract from other painful feelings or memories, or even feel alive in some way. Anyone who got that kind of relief would stay deeply invested in continuing the behaviors. They become an important resource for coping. And when you get relief in the short term, it makes it more likely that you will repeat the same behaviors in the future. Even when your loved ones or a therapist try to convince you that what you're doing is "bad for you," the behavior may be the only coping strategy you know and trust, and you will want to cling to it like a lifeline.

It's also confusing and complicated when well-meaning people in your life ask you to explain why you are doing something destructive. Many people who struggle with these behaviors can't explain to others why they feel the need to hurt themselves. This can create feelings of guilt, shame, and a self-diagnosis of being "weird" or "crazy." It also fuels a reaction of frustration, fear, or anger in others when there are no answers. Twenty-three-year-old Stephanie illustrates this when she says:

> My parents caught me throwing up—again—and this time they got really angry. They demanded to know why I keep doing this to myself. And the more they pushed, the more I realized I had no answer. That actually scared me a lot and made me realize how out of control this had become for me.

That's where this workbook can be helpful to you. Together we will explore—without judgment—the most common reasons why people do self-destructive behaviors. We will connect the behaviors to several specific experiences. It may relate to the challenges and changes that come with adolescence. It might be the result of having witnessed or experienced trauma, abuse, or neglect. Or it might be the byproduct of having an upsetting story to tell from life events or stressful experiences that haven't been resolved. I often refer to this as a "pain narrative." Connecting what you have been doing to the difficulties that go with being a teenager is useful because the beginning of adolescence is often associated with the start of self-destructive behaviors. That's not to say that only teenagers do these behaviors, or that it only begins in adolescence. Many people stumble upon self-destructive behaviors that seem to help them when they are much younger. And many people keep doing these behaviors well into older adulthood. But as you'll see, adolescence can be a particularly vulnerable time, partly because we are willing to take greater risks, so self-harm is often discovered around this age. Or there is an increase in existing destructive behaviors as teens attempt to cope with the additional stress that comes with being an adolescent.

Fifteen-year-old Artie has an alcoholic father and a mother who copes by "pretending Dad doesn't really have a problem." He helps us make the connection between self-destructive behavior and adolescence. You may relate to this if you are a teenager, or if you once felt this way when you were younger.

> When I was a kid I think it was easier to go along with my Mom's strategy. We downplayed my Dad's drinking and looked the other way so it didn't seem so bad. We tried to focus on the "good times" with Dad and ignored the bad times. But when I turned 13, I started to

feel so stressed by school. I felt insecure and thought that girls didn't like me. The added pressure made it harder and harder to ignore stuff at home. I needed another way to tune it out and not deal with it. I had experimented with pot when I was 11, but by the time I was 14 I was getting high everyday. It seemed like a better solution. When I was stoned nothing mattered, which was fine with me, because letting it matter hurt too much.

Later on we will explore in more detail the specific challenges of adolescence and how they often serve as "tipping points," causing teens to turn to self-destructive behaviors or up the ante with existing ones. It is certainly true that not everyone who has a problem with drugs, alcohol, eating, cutting, or sexual addictions has been abused or neglected in childhood. However, it is reasonable to assume that anyone who does those behaviors has an upsetting story to tell about something they experienced or witnessed that made them feel unsafe or betrayed their sense of trust. Typically this is an experience that cannot be expressed with words. And yet the person still needs to be comforted in some way. When something has interfered with their ability to self-soothe in healthy ways, they turn to destructive behaviors.

Traumatic experiences affect people in different ways, and some people can function at higher levels than others even with the effects of trauma. But any-one who has been through physical, emotional, psychological, verbal, or sexual abuse or some form of neglect pays a price and often suffers silently. There can be a big difference between an outer appearance of confidence and competence and inner feelings of inadequacy and shame. Sometimes trying to manage those opposite feelings creates more pain that needs to be soothed. Sometimes the resurfacing of painful or old memories and feelings needs to be pushed aside or comforted. Self-destructive acts can feel like a way to manage the leftover pain from these past traumatic or distressing experiences. Fifty-year-old Mary shows us this when she says:

I was a very successful businesswoman, who seemingly had it all! Everyone thought I had it together and probably would have been shocked and horrified to know that I was bingeing and purging almost nightly, and then crying myself to sleep. I felt haunted by memories of my grandfather inappropriately touching me. I felt dirty and damaged. It didn't matter how pretty or accomplished I was, that almost made it worse, because no one saw how much I was hurting or believed I could have such intense pain.

Future chapters will help you understand the importance of exploring the possible connection between self-destructive behaviors and prior traumatic or painful experiences. Identifying, working through, and resolving these "pain narratives" or painful life experiences, will eventually make the need to engage in self-destructive acts unnecessary for you.

One of the most important ideas I hope you get from this workbook is *what you have been doing makes sense given what you have experienced in the past.* We will look at these behaviors through a strengths-based, "de-stigmatized" lens. This means we will not look at these acts as signs of "mental illness" or "weakness." My belief is that these behaviors are creative coping strategies in response to very real emotional and psychological pain. Sometimes, they are the inevitable end result of that pain. This is especially true if you did not have any resources for comfort, love, and support. If no one was there to soothe you, you never learned how to self-soothe. And without that skill you resorted to anything that would make you feel better, even if, ironically, it also caused you pain. We will talk more about how being able to trust and feel safe with caretakers allows you to learn the skill of self-care. And we will also look at why it's so difficult to manage your emotions when you aren't allowed to feel a secure attachment to your caretakers.

Since you will be introduced to ideas that might be new to you, there is a glossary at the back of the book that will serve as a quick guide. When you come across a word or a concept that isn't familiar feel free to use the glossary to get a simple definition. Part of the healing journey is learning and embracing a new language that can put words to your experiences.

Another important part of this workbook relates to a "cycle" of self-destructive behavior and how that cycle repeats itself, making you do the behaviors over and over again. You'll learn about the impact of external things like "triggers" (experiences that remind you of painful things from the past) and internal processes like negative thoughts and feelings, increased anxiety and dissociation or "zoning out." You'll begin to understand how your body becomes conditioned to respond to stressful things with impulsive and compulsive acts that are self-destructive. This means you do something painful over and over again without really thinking about it, so the behavior becomes automatic.

Once you understand the "domino effect" of getting triggered you can begin to stop the cycle with other coping strategies that accomplish what self-harm has accomplished for you. This will give you back a genuine sense of *power and control*: two words that feel very important to people who hurt themselves. Only in this case, you can have the power and control without the negative fall-out of guilt, shame, secret keeping, or feeling weird or like a failure. Your new choices for coping and self-soothing will not threaten your job, your relationships, or undermine your physical, emotional, or psychological wellbeing.

Does this sound too good to be true? Feeling uncertain or doubtful is understandable. If you've been doing your self-destructive behaviors long enough you might think there are no other options. Again, I remind you that all that's needed to take this journey is courage and curiosity. And if you are still reading, you have both!

YOU ARE NOT IN THIS ALONE

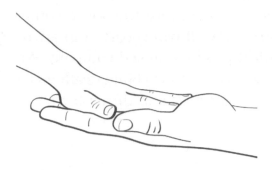

As you'll see, reading the chapters in this workbook is one way to gain new insights and understanding. In addition, since this is your own personal workbook, there will be many invitations to write, draw, try new behaviors, practice visualizations and guided imagery exercises. These are opportunities for you to work on a deeper level and to make the work more personal. As you find the courage to do so, you may find that different parts of the book bring up strong or overwhelming feelings for you. Therefore, after each exercise, it is very important that you take some time to comfort yourself and calm your body.

Although this workbook can be considered a resource for "self-help," I want to stress the value of doing this work with the support of a trained mental health professional. There are many reasons why working with a therapist, especially one who understands the impact of trauma, is really helpful and is strongly encouraged as you move forward in your healing journey.

Perhaps you have considered going to therapy but thought it wouldn't make a difference. Maybe you've had past experiences with mental health professionals and weren't happy with the results. Maybe your family, community, or cultural upbringing doesn't encourage reaching out for help or sharing your feelings with others. As you think about the idea of including therapy in your recovery plan, take a moment and respond to the following statements with your most honest thoughts and feelings. If you are currently seeing a therapist, address those statements as well.

JOURNAL EXERCISE: UNDERSTANDING YOUR FEELINGS ABOUT THERAPY

1) When I think about reaching out to a therapist for support and guidance, I think and feel:

_____

_____

_____

2) In general, my family's views about seeking outside help are:

_____

_____

_____

3) My culture's views about mental health and mental health professionals can be described as:

_____

_____

_____

4) If my family knew I was in therapy their reactions would be (or have been):

_____

_____

_____

5) Given my current or past experiences with therapy, my thoughts and feelings about working with a mental health professional include:

_____

_____

_____

Take a moment and notice what you've written, and see if anything feels new for you. Allow yourself to observe, without judgment, how you feel about your responses. Regardless of how you have responded, read on. The next few pages will either strengthen your instinct that therapy is extremely helpful or offer some new ideas about the advantages of doing this work with the support of a qualified mental health professional. This means someone who can explore the connection between your behaviors and PTSD, trauma, neglect, or painful past experiences while offering you new coping strategies that can help you resolve those issues.

Should you decide to include a therapist in your healing journey, or if you are already working with a therapist you trust, I'd like to suggest that you invite that clinician to read the book I wrote as a companion to this one entitled ***Treating Self-Destructive Behaviors in Trauma Survivors: A Clinician's Guide.*** It will echo and support all the ideas presented in this workbook and increase the likelihood that you and your therapist will be on the same page in terms of a strengths-based, non-"mental illness" approach to your coping strategies. They will be instructed on how to incorporate creative, non-judgmental treatment that can help to move your forward in your work.

The following chapter will give you a list of reasons why working with a qualified mental health professional can be helpful. Take your time reading the list and notice your responses. Give yourself permission to have an open mind as you move forward.

THE TOP TEN REASONS WHY A THERAPIST CAN HELP

1) Getting outside support breaks the cycle of handling pain alone

One of the most common reasons why people resist getting outside support is because they are already so used to dealing with their feelings and their overwhelming experiences by themselves. If you relate to this you might have never even thought that reaching out to others could be helpful. It might not even occur to you to ask for help. You may have grown up feeling alone or "invisible," because you were neglected, or you had overwhelmed, distracted, or unavailable caretakers who were unable to meet your needs. Maybe your needs and feelings were discounted, not valued, or ridiculed. At one point in time you may have tried to reach out, only to feel short-changed, misunderstood, not believed, or judged. As a result, you wisely stopped looking for outside help for comfort and support and recognized that you were "on your own." This became "normal" for you. You didn't want to go it alone—you simply had no choice. So you made the "best of it."

The idea of seeking out therapy may feel unnatural because it challenges your core belief about having to handle pain and conflicts by yourself. When you do find the courage to let a safe person support and guide you in your healing journey, you are breaking free from a powerful cycle of neglect. You are deciding to no longer accept the idea that you don't deserve help or that you must always go it alone. Managing life alone was never your idea in the first place, but it's what you were forced to do. You learned to totally rely on yourself in order to survive. Now you can learn to get support from others in order to thrive! And once you experience the comfort of being helped by a nurturing, safe therapist who truly "gets" what your self-destructive behaviors are about, you will be able to open your heart to the love and support of other safe people in your life as well.

Thirty-year-old Sara was an only child who grew up in a family with two very successful, high achieving parents. They often traveled for their jobs or spent hours away from home working with different community organizations. Sara struggled with depression and an eating disorder for most of her adolescence and adult life. Deciding to seek out treatment was a huge challenge for her.

> I never thought of myself as "neglected." We lived in a beautiful home, and I had every material thing I wanted. My parents were respected in the community. Everyone looked up to them and thought they were amazing people because they did so much to help others. It was "normal" for me to be home alone while they were out helping everyone else. If I had problems with school or boys I handled it myself. My parents loved me for being so self-sufficient. It never occurred to me to ask for help. When my eating disorder finally became unmanageable and I had to get help, it felt weird and foreign to reach out. I was actually proud of being self-sufficient until I realized it might not be normal to be totally self-sufficient as a kid. On a deeper level, I must have either assumed there would be no one around to help me, or that I didn't deserve it in the first place.

2) Therapy helps you see yourself and your situation from a different angle

The expression "you can't see the forest for the trees" applies to anyone overcome with negative thoughts and feelings. A therapist is able to "stand back" from those thoughts and feelings and provide you with a more objective, clear, and often more accurate take on your situation as well as your progress. You may be like many other people who tend to downplay their accomplishments as not important and exaggerate the seriousness of their mistakes. This is common in people who experience depression, anxiety, or have a history of unresolved painful experiences.

Or you may have people in your life who have fed you false information about your accomplishments or missteps. Sometimes we can't see ourselves in the same way that others see us because of self-esteem issues. If your siblings or parents felt threatened by your talents and strengths, they may have mocked you instead of encouraging your continued growth and healthy risk-taking. Oftentimes, people with low self-esteem feel threatened by another person's success. They might try to boost their own egos by putting down the people around them. They could also have given you the message that it is "selfish and egotistical" to think well of yourself, and this makes it impossible for you to accept accurate compliments about your abilities. In fact, being able to comfortably receive compliments is necessary for building confidence and self-worth.

With all of these damaging messages, seeing the glass as "half empty" becomes an automatic response. But automatic responses are often rooted in the past and aren't accurate reflections of current situations. An honest, objective therapist can help you sort out your automatic assumptions, separating the past from the present. He or she can help you look at your experience from a different angle, often showing you that the way you are seeing a current situation, measuring your progress, or assigning self-blame, needs to be looked at from a more objective point of view.

Twenty-five-year-old Bill was working on recovering from a sexual addiction. His behavior "soothed and numbed him" in the short term, and left him feeling "guilty and ashamed" in the long run. He commented on the importance of having an "objective witness" in therapy when he said:

> I never realized how hard I was on myself until I came in here and listened to the way YOU talk about what I'm doing. I beat myself up when I make a mistake and you see it as progress when I can pick myself up and move on. Like my parents, I focus on the fact that I fell down. But you focus on the fact that I got back up. We definitely see the same thing very differently! But if I'm honest about it, it feels a whole lot better and more hopeful to see it YOUR way!

3) Getting outside support breaks the cycle of secrecy and shame

If you are like so many people who use self-destructive behaviors to manage their distress, you know there is another exhausting and shaming part of the equation: trying to keep the behaviors hidden from everyone else in your life. This often results in having to invent and keep track of complicated lies, and lying only adds another layer of guilt. Keeping secrets adds fuel to the belief that there is something "wrong" with you or "bad" about you. Your lies may leave you feeling dishonest and fake, and that can lower your already fragile self-esteem. The ongoing fear of being "caught" or "found out" adds to your anxiety, which actually increases your "need" to soothe through destructive acts. Working with a therapist is a way to break the secrecy, and reduce the lying and guilty feelings.

It makes sense that you feel the need to lie and keep secrets as these are behaviors that get modeled and reinforced in dysfunctional families. Children are taught to keep secrets or lie about sexual abuse, domestic violence, addiction, and any other issue that is not being openly talked about within a family. Keeping secrets becomes a way to cope and survive and is "normalized" in families where grown-ups don't take responsibility for their actions, or don't want to deal with what's really happening. This becomes such a way of life that you may even have the experience of lying when you don't really have to: it just happens more automatically than telling the truth!

Forty-year-old Mary has been cutting her hands and arms for years. She never told anyone and spent most of her adult life trying to hide the behavior. Once she began therapy, she realized:

I've hated myself for two reasons—the fact that I cut myself and the fact that I lied about it. I've come up with every excuse you can think of, but I always feel cheap and dishonest. When I hear myself lying I hear my mother's voice. It's what she did my whole life. I don't think people actually believe my lies half the time. I have to say that it's starting to feel like a relief to not lie about my cutting in therapy. I can finally be honest and that helps to feel less guilty about it.

4) Therapy gives you the "cheerleader" you deserve

This is an idea that may be hard for you to believe or relate to when you think about what you actually deserve. It's possible that you haven't had too many "cheerleaders" in your life up until this point. Yet, we all need support and encouragement with no strings attached, especially when we are having trouble feeling optimistic or hopeful on our own. Repeated negative, frightening, or painful experiences as well as repeated relapses may have made it more difficult for you to believe in yourself, or to believe things can actually get better. A supportive, non-judgmental therapist can maintain a level of hope for you until you are able to feel it for yourself and believe it! A good therapist is also able to point out your progress, including the baby steps. Even when this positive feedback feels uncomfortable, it's important for you to experience someone praising you and taking pride in your growth. Eventually, you will be able to hold these positive messages inside and learn how to be your own best cheerleader.

In childhood you naturally turned to the adults you trusted to be your cheerleaders. It was normal and natural for you to seek out the love, approval, and attention of those caretakers. When they let you down, had strings attached to their praise, or were inconsistent or negative, you slowly learned to stop asking for and trusting their encouraging words. Keep in mind that if having a personal cheerleader seems uncomfortable, it's probably because this is a new experience for you. So if it feels awkward or confusing it's because it's a *new* experience, not because it's *wrong* or you don't deserve it.

Nineteen-year-old Catherine had been suffering from depression and used food and alcohol to self-medicate. She came into therapy "feeling like a failure" after relapsing several times. She began therapy with me and said the following after six months of treatment:

I actually used to dread it when you complimented me or got excited about something positive I did in therapy. It felt really uncomfortable, and I guess I was suspicious of it because no one else was complimenting me in my life. I thought you were just "acting" for my sake or because I pay you for therapy. Everyone in my life was always focused on the times I screwed up. There were moments in therapy when I needed to look away from you, and actually wanted to tell you to stop complimenting me. But over time it got easier, and now I can feel good when you say something nice. I sort of look forward to it! I even say to you, "you'll be proud of what I did this week" because I want you to be proud of me. I know that I still have to become my own cheerleader—that's harder—but I ask myself what *you* would say and then I can sort of say it to myself. I guess that's pretty good progress, huh?!

5) Therapy makes you more accountable for your actions

Doing this work by yourself is difficult because you won't have the same support, guidance, and encouragement. It's also really hard because it requires a level of self-discipline that is tough to maintain for anyone. The fact that you are reading this workbook means that you're interested in or at least curious about the possibility of changing your behavior. You may even tell yourself that you will change. Perhaps you have already attempted to let go of your self-destructive actions, only to fall back into the same patterns when you get stressed or overwhelmed.

As you recommit to this journey, you can choose between doing it the hard way or the easier way. I hope you will choose the easier way! That might feel like the unnatural choice because up until now things have always been so hard. But you deserve to do it the easier way, and when a therapist guides you through the process, you are more likely to follow through and accomplish your goals. Therapy can keep you honest and on track. When you know you have someone in your life who genuinely cares about your progress it can motivate you to actually *make* progress. Telling a trusted person that you plan to go to an A.A. meeting, take advantage of a resource, or practice new self-soothing behaviors will increase the likelihood that you will actually follow through with those healthier options because you will report back.

A therapist can also help make your goals specific, measureable, and doable. You're more likely to try a new behavior when it is clearly spelled out and presented in a positive way. "I have to stop hurting myself when I am stressed" might sound good, but it's vague, negative, and too broad. It would be hard to measure your success with this stated goal, and in all likelihood will eventually be forgotten because it is too overwhelming and unclear. But a therapist could "re-frame" or re-state that goal by giving you the homework assignment of "spending 15 minutes listening to soothing music and reading positive affirmations when you feel stressed," as a first concrete step towards moving you away from hurting yourself. This kind of assignment is useful because it's clear and measurable.

Seventeen-year-old Sam entered therapy with a strong desire to stop his substance abuse and self-mutilating behaviors. However, he didn't have a lot of family support, had tried repeatedly to "just stop" on his own, and always started it again when his anger got worse. He knew about Narcotics Anonymous meetings and kept telling himself to go, but never did. During the course of therapy he said:

> I honestly think that the only way I will finally go to an N.A. meeting is if I tell you I am going on a certain day and then have to come back to you next week to tell you whether or not I actually went. Telling myself I'm going doesn't seem to work, and I feel like my parents don't care if I go or not. I think you care and for some reason that makes a difference.

6) A therapist provides comfort and support when you relapse

When it comes to treating self-destructive behaviors, it's important to know that the work is often two steps forward and one step back. Relapsing can be a common part of the process. It's useful to know this, not to depress you, but rather to make it more normal for you. Almost everyone goes through some sort of "relapse" or setback when they are trying to let go of behaviors that used to be helpful and serve a purpose. And most people are likely to verbally beat themselves up when they do fall back on old behaviors. If you relate to this you'll understand how easy it is to think relapsing means "failing."

Ironically, the more you beat yourself up the more likely it is that you will do your self-destructive behavior again. This is because hurting yourself feels "right" when you feel badly about yourself. If you think of yourself as a "loser" or a "failure," then it makes sense that you "punish" your body rather than engage in self-care. With the support of a well-trained therapist you can think about these relapses as opportunities to learn and grow. As you compassionately revisit your self-destructive act, you can process the "triggers," or the things that set the relapse in motion, and brainstorm about what you could you have done differently. You can come up with a game plan for the next trigger, which prepares you for future incidents, making you less vulnerable and more able to respond in a healthier, more self-protective way.

Sixty-year-old Thomas was working on his sexual addiction and, in a moment of great loneliness, "relapsed" by going on Craigslist and having an unprotected sexual encounter with a stranger. He came into therapy feeling a lot of shame and "disgust," but was brave enough to process it with me. After we looked at his triggers, we came up with a new strategy to address his feelings of being lonely late at night, which included calling a therapeutic hotline to connect with someone in a healthier way rather than going on Craigslist or engaging in phone sex.

> You have no idea how much I was beating myself for doing this again. I really thought I was getting better, and then after I did this, I felt like I was back to square one. I was half expecting you to be mad at me, and I'm so relieved that you didn't judge me. After talking to you, I understand that not having another way to deal with my loneliness made me vulnerable to going on-line and looking for sex. It didn't occur to me to call a hotline, but it makes sense to try that next time.

7) A therapist can be your advocate with family and friends

As you may already know, self-destructive acts and the struggle to stop the behaviors are really hard to talk about with loved ones. They panic and get scared because they're desperate for you to stop, and they're worried that you will do permanent damage. They may get angry when you relapse, especially after you've promised them that you will stop. They may be confused and frustrated when you can't really explain why the behaviors still feel necessary or important to you. They may even take it personally, making you feel guilty and ashamed for "hurting or scaring them" by doing the behavior.

It is easy to get triggered by their reactions and a well-meaning conversation can turn out badly as your upset feelings increase and you get more defensive. A therapist who has an expertise in treating self-destructive behaviors can work with you to create an actual "script" you can use when loved ones ask about your behaviors. When you can express yourself in a less defensive way, the conversation is more likely to be productive. It's also useful to role-play with a therapist to identify your expectations, work out the rough edges, anticipate how loved ones might respond, and brainstorm about how to handle conflict when it arises. All of this planning will increase the possibility that you will communicate more effectively. Being able to express your needs and feelings with words, rather than through your acting-out behaviors is one of the overriding goals of treatment.

When you feel too overwhelmed or ashamed, your therapist should offer to be your voice, representing you to family and friends in a caring, non-judgmental way. This, in turn, increases the likelihood that other people can see you through the same caring lens. Concerned significant others might demand to know why your recovery is taking so long. They don't understand why you've relapsed again, and may think you're "not trying hard enough" or just don't care. A therapist who understands self-destructive behavior can set them straight, explaining that the recovery process doesn't happen quickly, isn't easy or straightforward. There will be many bumps in the road, and it's so important for your support system to not give up on you or your ability to eventually recover.

Fourteen-year-old Francine had been making deep scratches on her arms and legs since Middle School. Her parents pressured her about it, and on her own she had significantly reduced that behavior but was now starting to binge and purge instead. Her parents caught her doing her eating disordered behavior and when they demanded to know "how she could take such a giant step backwards and disappoint them again," she felt horribly ashamed and did not know how to respond. As I educated her about the common experience of replacing one behavior with another, she asked me to have a similar conversation with her parents.

They are so freaked out and they are making me feel worse about what I'm doing. I need you to tell them that I'm not totally hopeless. They are making me feel like I will never get better. Please explain that thing about replacing one kind of self-harm with another kind, so they know I am not doing it to hurt them. I can't explain it to them, I just freeze up when they ask me and then they get mad at me for not communicating with them.

8) A therapist can invite you to attach new meaning to your experiences

If you are like a lot of people, you may get "tunnel vision" about the painful things you've been through. This means you have a limited view of yourself, what has happened to you, and your existing repertoire of coping strategies. Sometimes, the meaning you attach to your experiences is almost more important than the experience itself, because the way you think about things profoundly influences how you feel and the behavioral choices you make. It's easy to get stuck in a narrow, negative view of yourself and your life, and when you attach certain meanings to your experiences you can actually add another layer of trauma.

The following are some examples of how the meaning you bring to something can make the event more traumatic and harder to resolve. If you "personalize" the experience (believe it's all about you), feel "targeted," singled out, or feel like the world is out to get you that will make it worse. If you believe you could have or should have stopped or prevented trauma from occurring, feel responsible for the event, or think it was somehow your fault, you are more likely to feel depressed, anxious, helpless, and hopeless. If you believe that your pain or your self-destructive behaviors are evidence that you are "bizarre," or "sick," it will keep you isolated and ashamed.

A therapist can offer you a different perspective, which gives you another way to think about the same event. Therapy can help you recognize that the abuse wasn't your fault and that there wasn't anything you could have done to stop it or prevent it. Therapy can help you focus on the fact that you survived and you can use your experiences as an opportunity to connect with others, personally grow, and even make a difference in the world. That new perspective can create feelings of gratitude, appreciation, optimism, an increased sense of faith, a desire to connect with others, and the belief that you've been given a second chance to thrive. It makes sense that you would need the guidance of an objective and supportive therapist to see your experiences in this new light, and it is a gift to be given this new mindset.

Fifty-year-old Marjorie had spent most of her life believing that her childhood physical and sexual abuse was her fault, and saw it as "evidence" that she was "worthless." Her perpetrators convinced her that she "wanted and deserved" the trauma and terrible treatment she experienced. Her self-blame left her feeling hopeless, and in her mind, it justified bingeing to the point of obesity and diabetes, cutting her torso, and staying married to an emotionally abusive partner. As her therapy unfolded and she slowly learned to attach new meaning to her trauma she said:

As horrible as my abuse was, I'm seeing that the way I talked to myself about it was just as damaging. As long as I believed that I deserved it, it made sense to keep treating myself like crap and to let my husband treat me that way, too. Now I have my moments of thinking that maybe I didn't do anything to deserve my childhood abuse, and maybe I'm not such a loser. Maybe I'm not destined to spend the rest of my life in a bad marriage—maybe I can actually be happy one day.

9) Working with a therapist gives you a witness for your painful experiences

I believe that everyone wants a witness for personal pain. Even when you have been forced to keep things a secret, there is a natural desire to share your experiences with people who are safe and compassionate. Hurting your body is like standing on top of a mountain and screaming your experience in Greek. The problem is no one around you speaks Greek. Therefore, they focus on the fact that you are screaming and they want you to stop! The creative ways in which you are trying to "show" what you are unable to "tell" are misunderstood by those around you who only focus on what you are doing and not the message underneath the behavior. And since you are doing things that seem scary and dangerous to others, they are even more focused on trying to stop the behavior without taking the time to hear why and how the behavior speaks to you and represents your pain narrative.

A therapist who supports the treatment perspectives in this workbook can help "translate" your behaviors and de-code your communication so you finally feel heard, understood, and supported. Part of why you do what you do is to get the people around you to witness or see your pain. You may be saying that you feel your body is "damaged," "dirty," or "bad" (by cutting or burning it). You may be showing the world that you feel invisible, or you didn't get enough nurturance (by starving) or that you need a protective shield around you to feel safe (by gaining a lot of weight). Perhaps you were taught to connect attachment and love with a sexual violation (by engaging in unsafe sexual behaviors). Or you want the world to know that zoning out, dissociating, or getting high is the only way you know how to escape emotional pain.

When you work with a therapist who "gets it," and can non-judgmentally bear witness to your experiences, the need to act them out by hurting yourself will dramatically decrease for you. A trained therapist can also give you safer, alternative ways to "tell" your story, so others can bear witness as well.

Twenty-two-year-old Charity had been hospitalized several times for starving herself and losing a significant amount of weight. Her hospital stays were always about "getting her to goal weight" so she could be discharged. No one looked deeper to understand what Charity was trying to "communicate" through her anorexia. In therapy we began to connect starving with feeling invisible at home and wanting her parents to know how emotionally neglected she felt, given the fact that they were preoccupied with her heroin-addicted sister. She started to realize how her actions were not really getting her anywhere when she said:

> All my parents were focused on was my weight loss, and they assumed the hospital would fix that. They didn't understand—and I didn't understand—that I was "talking in code," trying to show them how alone and invisible I felt. And the more they "didn't get it" the more weight I lost. I guess I kept upping the ante, hoping that sooner or later they would

stop focusing on my sister and finally give me the attention I was craving. But I didn't want the attention to be focused on my eating disorder. I just wanted to feel like they loved me as much as they loved my sister and to believe that they were there for me.

10) Therapy can offer you creative new ways to think about and work with your symptoms

If you are like most people who use self-destructive behaviors, the diagnosis you have probably given yourself is "weird," "sick," or "hopeless." If you feel the need to hurt your body or engage in other destructive acts and don't understand why, then these self-diagnoses are an attempt to make sense out of what you're doing. A well-trained therapist who supports this approach to self-destructive behaviors can give you a whole new way to think about your actions. They can be connected to your family-of-origin, the possibility of prior abuse, neglect or trauma, the challenges of adolescence or another developmental milestone or life stressor you may have experienced.

A therapist can also introduce the concept of "meta-communication," which is the non-verbal expression of your feelings and needs. This will help you connect what you are doing to a specific pain narrative that you might not yet have the words to verbally explain. For example, you might engage in unprotected, unsafe sex because you are communicating the same lack of respect for your body that an abuser demonstrated when he or she hurt you. A therapist can move you away from the hopelessness of a diagnosis like "borderline" (which is often automatically attached to acts of self-injury) and help you to re-frame your symptoms as the inevitable byproducts of trauma or pain. This restores a sense of hope into the work and takes the glass ceiling off of your progress!

There are many therapists who work with self-destructive behaviors, and there are varying schools of thought about how to best treat these issues. Some therapists are strong believers in safety contracts, and some are quick to hospitalize clients who relapse or don't progress quickly enough. I want to emphasize that I am not judging those practitioners, and certainly client safety is of the upmost importance. I am simply offering a model that I have found to be helpful and one that has benefitted many clients. There is no such thing as the "perfect clinician." And some of these behaviors can feel very challenging to treat. However, I encourage you to seek out a therapist who can keep an open mind about treatment options, and who recognizes the value of focusing on your strengths, resiliency, and creativity. If you are considering going to a therapist don't be afraid to ask them how they intend to work with the behaviors, what they have found most useful, whether or not they use safety contracts, or how often they hospitalize their clients.

One of the most important byproducts of doing this work in therapy is that it gives you the tools to find other ways to express yourself and comfort yourself. We will explore, in future chapters, how to incorporate artwork, journaling, and other strategies that let you "show" your experiences safely rather than re-enacting them on your body. You will also learn how to self-soothe in genuinely comforting ways rather than numbing or re-traumatizing yourself. Although you will be able to do some of that right here in this workbook, processing it with a compassionate guide can make your recovery more meaningful and more lasting.

Seventy-five-year-old Martin had, by all accounts, "a good life." He had a loving family, was successful in his career, and was still in good physical health. Two years ago, his wife of over 50 years died suddenly and Martin's world was "turned upside down." He was overcome with grief, but "didn't want to burden his adult children so he pretended he was fine." Unable to cope, he turned to alcohol and video games to escape.

I really thought I was losing my mind, and didn't know how else to drown my pain, so drinking became the escape. I don't know how it happened, but suddenly I was spending up to eight hours a day playing video games by myself on the home computer. I thought I was going crazy, but I realize in talking to you that this was an escape, too. Playing video games until I won and beat every level, gave me back a sense of power and control that I lost when my wife suddenly died. You're helping me to see that I do need to be comforted and numbing my pain won't really help. Maybe I'll start going to that support group you suggested.

After reading about the potential benefits of working with a well-trained mental health provider, take a moment and respond to the following statement:

With an open mind and an open heart, I can list the ways in which I could continue to benefit from either staying in therapy or finding the courage to seek out a therapist at this time:

_____

_____

_____

_____

_____

_____

_____

_____

_____

_____

_____

_____

_____

_____

_____

_____

Remember this workbook is not meant to be a substitute for therapy. If you are still not yet convinced of the value of doing this work with professional support, and you want to continue reading, please consider the following suggestions. They are designed to keep the work safe for you by reducing the likelihood that you will become "flooded" which means emotionally overwhelmed and not able to manage your experiences.

Pace yourself carefully. This means it's important to do the work slowly over time, rather than rushing through it. Read a little and then stop. Notice how you are feeling emotionally. Notice the body sensations, thoughts, and images that may have come to the surface as a result of something you read or wrote. Take the time to stop, rest, and re-group rather than plowing ahead. In the long run you will be able to do more work if you do it slowly.

Have some resource for support. Even if you choose not to use a therapist, think about reaching out to a relative, friend, teacher, 12 step sponsor, a safe and supportive chat room, or member of the clergy. Without sharing personal details, let them know you are working on important, difficult issues and you may need an extra hug, more time to just be in their company, a listening ear, or a friend to do something fun. If it still feels too scary to connect with another person consider using a 24-hour hotline. It's a way to feel supported while keeping your identity and feelings private. Most hotline workers are well trained and non-judgmental. They can help to re-ground you or comfort you, even in the middle of the night!

Have a healthy, creative outlet to help you unwind. Look for a way to balance the intensity of this work by doing something creative and fun that can calm you, empower you, or help you take a break when you need it. Doing something physical can help release tension. Doing something productive can increase your sense of competence. Doing something creative or playful can lighten your mood and reduce feelings of depression or anxiety. As you prepare for the journey in this workbook, consider things like finding a good yoga studio, having inspiring literature available, taking up or re-visiting a simple but fun hobby, signing up for a few massages, getting a guided imagery CD for relaxation, stocking up on great smelling candles.

Stay open to the possibility that down the road, reaching out to a therapist may be helpful. You are allowed to change your mind at any time during this process. The more deeply you go into this subject, the more you may realize that there are other, more hidden layers that are deserving of additional support or outside help.

Even if you are doing the work with a therapist, pay attention to points 1, 2, and 3 and be sure to use them as you move forward with this workbook. You have plenty of time, and the goal is to do the work comfortably and safely!

4

IS THIS WORKBOOK REALLY
RIGHT FOR ME?

It would be natural to question whether or not this workbook truly relates to your situation and your behaviors. It's meaningful that you were drawn to it in the first place. There may have been something in the title that caught your attention, and that's something you should trust. But if you are like most people who depend on self-destructive behaviors, you may go back and forth between thinking it's a problem and wanting to decrease or stop it, and then getting cold feet and talking yourself back into believing that "it's not so bad," or you "have it under control."

If you already relate to anything you've read, know that you are on the right track. If you are still unsure, let's give you another opportunity to decide whether or not this workbook is right for you. The main questions you need to answer are:

Do you use self-destructive behaviors?

How do they "help" you?

Do those behaviors wind up creating problems for you in your life?

When you feel ready, take some time and fill out this three-part questionnaire. You don't have to answer the questions all at one time. In fact, it's helpful to pause in between each questionnaire, stand up, stretch, and do some deep breathing. Try to answer the questions as honestly as you can. You don't need to share the answers with anyone else. This exercise is not meant to shame you in any way. It is meant to give you insight, so you can make an educated decision about whether or not to go forward with the work at this time. There are no scores with these questionnaires. Use your answers as a "roadmap" to help you figure out and understand the role that self-harm plays in your life.

1) IDENTIFYING MY SELF-DESTRUCTIVE BEHAVIORS

Put a check mark next to any and all of the behaviors you have ever done, and in the space provided write down how often you do that behavior. You can also indicate if you are currently doing the behavior, or have done it in the past. There is blank space on the bottom to list any other ways you may be self-harming that are not included in the questionnaire.

*In the questionnaire, the word **excessive** means engaging in the behavior to the point where it interferes with or creates problems for you at work, in school, with your legal status, in relationships, or your health.

___ restricting calories or starving _____
   ___ in the past ___ currently

___ bingeing on food _____
   ___ in the past ___ currently

___ purging by making yourself vomit _____
   ___ in the past ___ currently

___ purging through laxative abuse or enemas _____
   ___ in the past ___ currently

___ purging through excessive exercise _____
   ___ in the past ___ currently

___ using illegal drugs _____
   ___ in the past ___ currently

___ abusing prescription drugs _____

   in the past ___ currently

___ excessive use of alcohol _____
   ___ in the past ___ currently

___ cutting any part of your body _____
   ___ in the past ___ currently

___ burning any part of your body _____
   ___ in the past ___ currently

___ pulling hair anywhere on your body _____
   ___ in the past ___ currently

___ limb banging or bruising _____
   ___ in the past ___ currently

___ inserting objects in body openings (vagina, anus, nose) _____
___ in the past ___ currently

___ other acts of self-mutilation or injuring the body _____
___ in the past ___ currently

___ engaging in unprotected or unsafe sexual activity _____
___ in the past ___ currently

___ engaging in sexual addiction _____
___ in the past ___ currently

___ engaging in pornography or cybersex addiction _____
___ in the past ___ currently

___ engaging in excessive masturbation _____
___ in the past ___ currently

___ engaging in compulsive gambling _____
___ in the past ___ currently

___ engaging in compulsive shopping or spending _____
___ in the past ___ currently

___ engaging in Internet or video game addiction _____
___ in the past ___ currently

___ engaging in reckless driving _____
___ in the past ___ currently

___ engaging in shoplifting _____
___ in the past ___ currently

___ other self-destructive behaviors _____
___ in the past ___ currently

2) UNDERSTANDING HOW MY SELF-DESTRUCTIVE BEHAVIORS SEEM TO HELP ME IN THE SHORT TERM

People use self-destructive behaviors for many different reasons. Take a moment to read the following list of common reasons and circle Y (yes) if the statement applies to you and N (no) if it does not. Feel free to include additional reasons under "other".

Y   N   1) to stop feeling so bad or so tense

Y   N   2) to "take away" upsetting thoughts

Y   N   3) to feel more in control of my body

Y   N   4) to make invisible inside wounds, outside and visible

Y   N   5) to create the opportunity and a reason to engage in self-care

Y   N   6) to "show" earlier trauma experiences

Y   N   7) to stop myself from telling something about my trauma story

Y   N   8) to get revenge

Y   N   9) to outwardly express anger that I hold inside

Y   N   10) to mark a certain occasion or event so I can remember it

Y   N   11) to punish myself for behaviors I think are "sinful" or "bad"

Y   N   12) to cry out for help

Y   N   13) to check out, dissociate, or feel numb

Y   N   14) to return to reality or stop feeling "out of it"

Y   N   15) to feel safer and more secure

Y   N   16) to feel unique, special, or different

Y   N   17) to feel "a rush"

Y   N   18) to achieve a sense of identity

Y   N   19) to reconnect with myself and feel whole or alive

Y   N   20) to stimulate myself

Y   N   21) to "purify" or "cleanse" my body

Y   N   22) to distract myself from something or someone threatening

Y   N   23) as a way for my alters or other "personalities" to communicate

Y   N   24) to feel peaceful or calm

Y   N   25) to punish or control other people

Y   N   26) to get others to connect with me

Y   N   27) to show how much I hate myself

Y   N   28) to get attention from someone important in my life

Y   N   29) to leave a mark so people know my pain is real

Y   N   30) to show others my pain without words

Other reasons: _____

_____

_____

_____

_____

3) HOW THESE BEHAVIORS MAY NOT HELP IN THE LONG TERM

As you know, self-destructive behaviors can give you a temporary feeling of relief, of "owning" your body or getting back a feeling of "control." However, as you notice the behaviors you've identified above, allow yourself, without judgment, to consider if these behaviors ever lead to **negative** consequences. Check off any and all that apply. Take your time reading and responding to the statements.

___ the behavior creates tension with family members

___ the behavior creates tension with my significant other

___ loved ones are often angry at me

___ loved ones are often afraid of what I am doing

___ I feel afraid of myself

___ I am mad at myself a lot

___ I feel hopeless or depressed about my ability to stop or get better

___ I am often anxious because of my behaviors

___ I often have to hurt myself more to get the same effect

___ my job performance is negatively affected

___ my relationship with co-workers suffers

___ the behavior creates health risks or medical problems

___ the behavior leaves me physically unsafe

___ the behavior creates legal problems for me

___ the behavior negatively affects my school performance

___ I feel more isolated and disconnected from friends

___ I feel more isolated or disconnected from family

___ the behavior negatively affects my finances

___ the behavior prevents me from reaching certain life goals

___ the behavior has cost me a personal relationship

___ the behavior negatively affects my ability to parent my children

___ the behavior negatively affects my self-esteem and self-worth

___ the behavior traumatizes me

___ the behavior forced me to be hospitalized

___ the behavior has landed me in prison

___ I have lost personal possessions because of it

___ the behavior prevents me from being intimate with others

___ I spend a lot of time hiding things, keeping secrets, or lying

___ the behavior led me to commit a crime

___ the behavior causes sleep disturbances

___ the behavior leaves me feeling guilty or ashamed

___ the behavior leaves me feeling powerless and out of control

___ the behavior leaves me feeling like a "failure"

___ the behavior causes others to disapprove of or reject me

___ the behavior leaves me feeling like a victim

Other consequences: _____

_____

_____

_____

_____

Answering these questions is a big step, so you may be feeling anxious or upset now. There are many self-soothing strategies that you will learn about in Part IV of the workbook, but here are a few ideas to get you started in case you find any of the beginning exercises upsetting. If you try a strategy and find that it doesn't work or doesn't feel right, always give yourself permission to stop and try something else! Sometimes, just doing a little bit of the strategy or coming back to it another time can be helpful, too.

*Sit quietly and take a few slow, deep breaths. As you inhale say a word in your mind that calms you, and as you exhale say another word that you find comforting. Make sure you fully exhale.

*Put on soothing music, hug a pillow, and gently rock.

*Stand up and stretch or "shake it off" by swinging your arms and legs.

*Make yourself a cup of tea or hot cocoa and read positive affirmations that you have downloaded from the Internet.

*Spend a few minutes watching an enjoyable or funny video from YouTube.

*Take some time to pray or have a conversation with a higher power.

*Take a short walk and make a mental note of the things you see, hear, smell, or feel.

*Rest in the grass or sit in a comfortable chair outside and blow bubbles.

*Give yourself a hand massage with your favorite lotion.

*Cuddle a favorite pet.

Remember—your answers are meant to give you insight and help you to move forward, not depress, shame, or anger you. When you can, compassionately re-visit your answers and use them to decide whether or not this workbook is right for you. Know that you can find the courage to accept it if you do engage in self-harming acts and they create negative consequences for you. The good news is, you have taken another step forward in your healing journey and are that much closer to fully letting go of the patterns that hold you hostage and keep you stuck.

PART II

CONNECTING SELF-DESTRUCTIVE BEHAVIORS TO PAST AND PRESENT EXPERIENCES

5

IT'S NOT EASY BEING A TEENAGER OR AN ADULT!

In this chapter, we will look at the challenges of being an adolescent and how those stressors can lead to self-destructive behaviors. It's worth reading this part if you are currently a teenager as it will help your struggles feel more "normal." It's also worth reading this section even if you are an adult because it will probably put your feelings into a historical background and shed some light on where you've been. We will also look at the stressors that are unique to older adults since self-harming behaviors can continue well into the later part of your life.

The Stressors of Adolescence

There are differences between the adolescents and young adults who self-harm and have traumatic backgrounds and the groups of adolescents who superficially do non-suicidal self-injury (NSSI). The dynamics associated with NSSI can be quite different than the underlying motives associated with people who self-harm more frequently and do more serious damage to their bodies. If you are an adolescent and have "tried" non-suicidal self-injury you may be engaging in the behavior for other reasons. You might be "experimenting" to fit in with your peers. When more kids start doing self-injurious behaviors in a school setting or a psychiatric inpatient setting, some people assume it's just contagious behavior: kids doing it because other kids do it. There is research about this, but no clear evidence to prove that this is the reason why schools are seeing an increase in the behaviors.

If you are a teenager who occasionally does mild forms of self-harm, you may feel like it's a way to test your "courage," or you might be imitating popular media personalities who talk about—even brag about—their eating disorders, addictions, and self-mutilating behaviors as a way to manage their emotional pain. You might be acting out impulsively, from poor judgment or aggression. Those features don't mean you are bad. They are actually strongly associated with your developing "adolescent brain."

You may know teenagers who secretly get support for their attempts at self-harm, as well as "guidance" about how to self-injure by looking at websites and on-line videos that make cutting and starving behaviors seem normal or even romantic. Sadly, it is so easy to access detailed information about how to "safely" cut or handle the physical pain of starvation, and this may account for an increase in the behavior amongst certain curious teenagers.

Much has been written about teenagers who experiment with cutting, burning, purging, and substance abuse. It is almost presented as a "normal" and necessary "rite of passage." Having worked with many teenagers who engage in these behaviors, I strongly believe that it is a mistake to think about these behaviors as "typical experimentation." Self-destructive behaviors can all serve similar purposes: they help you manage your emotions in the short term by soothing you through distracting, numbing, or releasing chemicals in your brain called endorphins, which make you feel better. Hurting your body is a way to seek out attention, empathy, and help from concerned friends or unavailable, preoccupied adults. If you, a friend or a family member are "experimenting" with these kinds of acts, the rest of us have an ethical responsibility to ask ourselves, "Why does this behavior 'make sense' to this person?" "What is going on in their life or inside of them that would explain why they are deliberately creating physical or emotional pain or discomfort?"

Therefore, I disagree with the idea that you are hurting yourself strictly because it is "contagious" behavior. This is not like mimicking the fashion or hairstyle of the "cool kids." These are dangerous, sometimes painful, and often scary behaviors that "speak to you" or a loved one for very specific reasons. In future chapters you will learn why self-destructive acts might "speak to you" and you'll see why this is a critical part of eventually being able to let go of the behavior.

Interestingly, body piercings and tattoos are often thought to be acts of self-harm when they are not. The critical distinction is that teens often do these things because they believe it makes their bodies more beautiful. They are motivated by a genuine belief that metal studs in their tongues, spikes in their lips and eyebrows, as well as all kinds of permanent images imprinted on their skin make their bodies look *better*. When adolescents are engaging in self-harm, it is something they do to their own bodies, it is often shame-based, isolating, and certainly not about enhancing the body cosmetically.

If you do have multiple tattoos or a lot of piercings, think about what motivates you to get pierced and tattooed. And think about the meaning you attach to the images you put on your skin. Do they somehow connect to your personal story of pain or suffering? Images like broken hearts, eyes with tears, daggers with dripping blood, objects penetrating other things, caged or trapped animals or people are possible examples of tattoos that have a deeper meaning and are related to unresolved trauma and pain. If you get piercings, do you let them get infected and then pick at the scabs? If you do, this becomes a more self-destructive act.

If you are a teenager who does self-harming behaviors, but feel strongly that you were not abused or neglected, there may be other reasons why hurting the body speaks to you. Oftentimes, there is an untapped painful story that has not been expressed with words. This might connect to the difficult challenges of figuring out your identity: a task that all adolescents go through but one that is sometimes very confusing and painful. Another major adolescent challenge is dealing with complicated and stressful peer relationships. As you try to manage these complex issues, you may not have support to openly discuss your feelings and experiences. Since you still need to process what is happening, you may begin expressing your complicated feelings through self-destructive behaviors.

Even Marcia Brady in the "Brady Bunch," or a teenage character from any sitcom about the "perfect" family, has days when they struggle with low self-worth, tension, and problems with friends, boyfriends, and family members, school pressures, and distress over body changes. Versions of disappointing and upsetting experiences can happen in the lives of all teenagers. However, in the case of these teenagers on T.V., there are loving and available resources to help with difficult experiences. Wise adults can challenge thoughts that are inaccurate or negative, help problem solve, provide comfort, and give a sense of hope and optimism by re-framing the pain as time-limited.

As we've already discussed, unlike Marcia Brady, you may have been or still are a teenager who was forced to deal with life's challenges alone. You may have figured out that your emotionally and/or physically unavailable caretakers would not be there to lend support, guidance, wisdom, or encouragement. Another major difference is that Marcia Brady grew up in simpler times; the kinds of conflicts and decisions she faced were relatively tame compared to the options, conflicts, and choices that teenagers currently face. Let's take a closer look at some of what teenagers have to juggle and deal with in today's society.

Aside from the very first year of life, we experience the most physical and brain-based changes during adolescence. Puberty is the biological process of intense change: the body gets redefined in shape, size, and hormonal structure. For many adolescents, these shifts are unwanted and confusing and can result in something I call "body betrayal." Rather than celebrating these newfound changes, male and female teenagers can resent their bodies, connecting their lack of popularity, poor athletic ability, or average academic performance to being too tall, overly developed, hairy or pimpled, under-weight, or over-weight. Many teenagers have experienced the embarrassment of an unexpected menstrual cycle, an erection that wouldn't go away quickly enough, or being teased for their looks.

Forty-seven-year-old Richard, who has struggled with intimacy issues, a dependence on marijuana, and sexual addiction, shows us the concept of "body betrayal" when he talks about a devastatingly traumatic experience that began in 8th grade:

When I was in middle school, I had a gorgeous young math teacher. One day, at the end of class, the bell rang to dismiss us for lunch. Almost all of the kids got up and ran out of the room. I had a full-blown erection and couldn't move. I felt ashamed and terrified. I remember two of my friends trying to push me out of my seat to get to the lunchroom. I was so embarrassed about my erection and I tried to make excuses about why I couldn't get up. One of my friends saw it and started teasing me about it. The teacher came over and saw it too. I wanted to die. I hated myself, hated my body. Word spread and I was teased about that through 12th grade. I never let go of those feelings of hating my body. No wonder I abused it for years afterwards!

This speaks to a powerful idea that was mentioned earlier: if you hate your body then it will become acceptable to hurt it. It also reminds us of how damaging teasing can be for teenagers, especially when they are already insecure. And in today's culture you know that the teasing is not limited to the school hallway or the gym locker room. Cyber-bullying can be overwhelming and deeply traumatizing for many kids. It is impossible to "take back" what is thrown into cyberspace and the speed with which rumors get passed around is mind-boggling. Rather than taking out their anger or rage on other people, many kids who are teased hold these experiences inside of themselves, blaming the "flaws" and "inadequacies" of their own bodies for the mocking they experience from peers. Sadly, kids growing up in profoundly dysfunctional families may get additional teasing at home when uncaring siblings or cruel parents think it is acceptable or funny to make crude comments about their developing bodies.

As stated earlier, when you are a teenager you are very focused on figuring out your identity, and this is accomplished, in large part, by your success in joining peer groups and feeling like you are accepted and belong. Therefore, it can be devastating when your best friends suddenly ignore you or your peer group seems to reject you for no reason. It is unfair that self-esteem and self-worth can be compromised by unpredictable peer relationships, but it is often the case.

Since acceptance means so much, many teenagers feel they have to look a certain way in order to fit in. The idea that there is a "right way" and a "wrong way" to look is strongly promoted by our culture. Many teens are influenced by the images in fashion and gossip magazines, CD covers, 20- and 30-year-old movie stars who get plastic surgery and botox, actors with six-pack abs who go on talk shows complaining about how "out of shape they are," and teen Internet sites that award modeling contracts to girls who should be hospitalized for anorexia. We are a society that loves beautiful, young, and thin, and teenagers are very tuned in to this reality. If you already struggle with self-consciousness, low self-esteem, or occasional feelings of worthlessness, the difference between your body shape and facial features versus the images of make-believe perfection that you see on T.V. and in the movies can create the "tipping point" that makes self-destructive behaviors an option.

In addition to the almost obsessive emphasis that is placed on body image and the desperate need to "fit in" with their peers, today's adolescents are faced with many other stressors. At very young ages they are being asked to make difficult and complicated decisions about becoming sexually active, substance use, cheating in school, shoplifting, or driving with a friend who is drunk or doesn't have a license. They are pressured to succeed academically, choose their future careers at younger ages, juggle many extra-curricular activities, build impressive resumes before graduating from High School, and even work part-time to help out with the family's troubled finances.

Eleven-year-old Tammy illustrates how hard it is to be a young teen in today's world when she suddenly says at the end of a session:

> So, a lot of my friends said it would be a good idea for me to "do it" with Jared at lunchtime in the bathroom. I mean not sex or anything, just like a blowjob or a hand job so he knows I like him. I just don't want him to film it on his phone or try to put it on the Internet 'cause I know my parents might see it. They also said if I did it, it would help me get in with the more popular group and I really want to hang out with them. So, like, do you think I should? I kind of want to if it would get me invited to their parties.

How sad that an 11-year-old would even think about this kind of behavior in order to "fit in." And notice that 11-year-old Tammy didn't think "a blowjob or a hand job" was sex. Sadly, her concern about Jared filming it on his phone was connected to a fear of her parents finding out, not an awareness that his behavior would be a terrible violation of trust or privacy. All of these things take a toll, and even in the absence of abuse, these are the issues that are creating "pain narratives" for teenagers like you in today's world.

Even when you are aware of the more obvious sources of stress, sometimes there are additional issues that effect self-harming behaviors. These might include the frustration of undiagnosed learning differences, issues with organizational skills, ADD, and the emotional or physical unavailability of parents and adult supervision. Many teenagers walk around with undiagnosed and untreated depression and anxiety and this, too, increases the "need" to engage in self-harming behaviors as a way to self-soothe and self-medicate.

If Marcia Brady was faced with these complications, it's possible she would go to her housekeeper, Alice, for advice, if not a parent. Today, many successful parents are traveling, attending Board meetings, working late, spending evening hours on the Internet, or sadly, remain out of touch with their teenagers' emotional needs.

The family dynamics in 15-year-old Tracie's home show the consequences of being raised by emotionally or physically unavailable parents:

> At first it was fun to invite a bunch of kids over whenever my parents were away, which happened a lot. I got really popular and my house was known as the "party house." But then kids started having sex and bringing alcohol and heroin into the house and I didn't know what to do. They didn't listen when I asked them to stop, so then I started drinking and doing heroin, too. Partly because it looked like fun, partly because I didn't want them to be mad at me or make fun of me if I didn't do it. But there were times when I wished my parents would come home sooner, even if it meant they would be angry. I just wanted them to take over, kick the kids out. Just handle it for me. Then I started to get high even more so I wouldn't feel how angry I was at my parents for not being there.

Without realizing it, you may also be affected by an over-exposure to violence and sexuality on the Internet and in video games. Spending countless hours staring at computer screens can actually put you into a kind of hypnotic or dissociative state. Watching violent interactions and passive/dominant pornography or video games reinforces that it's ok to hurt the body. And when you already "zone out" a lot, spending excessive amounts of time on-line and staring at computers may also put you at increased risk for self-harm. This is because it increases your sense of disconnection from your own body, and the more you space out, the easier it is to inflict physical pain upon yourself.

If you are a teenager, through no fault of your own, you are a part of a generation that struggles with social and communication skills because everything is texted or e-mailed. Although this can definitely make life easier, there may be negative long-term effects from reduced "face to face" time. How many of the hundreds of Facebook "friends" are actually your close friends? What's the impact that cyber-relationships have on your need for social engagement, attachment, safe touch, and ongoing intimacy in relationships? If your connections are all done at a distance and remain impersonal, it's hard to truly build trust and feel genuinely close to others.

In early childhood, using soothing strategies such as a pacifier, sucking your thumb, holding a stuffed animal or blanket, or sitting in the lap of a safe caretaker would give you the comfort and support you needed. In adolescence, most of these strategies are embarrassing and not socially acceptable, so you need other ways to self-soothe. If there are no consistent, healthy, available resources, then self-destructive behaviors become an option. The irony is many parents believe that as their children get older, they require less and less supervision and hands-on parenting. As a teenager who is trying to appropriately separate from parents, you might send out mixed messages about your desire for independence and privacy.

But in your most honest moments, you would probably admit that the world is sometimes a scary place, and despite wanting your separateness and freedom, there are times when you don't really know what you're doing yet. You still want and need guidance. What you are being asked to deal with requires wisdom, objectivity, the ability to analyze and see things from many different perspectives, as well as understanding the "cause and effect" of your actions. *Those abilities are literally not yet fully wired in an adolescent brain,* and as a result, you still actually need a tremendous amount of guidance and support.

It's important to know that the adolescent brain is still impulsive, aggressive, pleasure seeking, wants instant gratification, and engages in high-risk behaviors. You can see how the adolescent brain could make a teenager vulnerable to self-destructive acts! However, when the safety net of adult supervision and support is in place those same qualities can be properly channeled and teenagers can be spontaneous, passionate about causes, creative, adventurous, willing and eager to try new things and to dream big dreams.

DRAWING EXERCISE: EXPLORING ADOLESCENT STRESSORS

A) In the space below, using line, shape and color—either in concrete images or just "scribbling"—see if you can draw something that represents some of the adolescent stressors you currently experience, or experienced in the past.

B) Now in the space below, using line, shape and color—either in concrete images or just "scribbling"—see if you can draw something that can shift the image so you can bring some soothing or hope to the picture.

The Stressors of Adulthood

Although adolescence is a vulnerable time and can be traumatizing for many teens there are other challenges that happen as you go through different life stages. These normal milestones and occasional stumbling blocks can create intense feelings of anxiety, fear, inadequacy, anger, depression, helplessness, and even shame. If you are lacking in good resources for comfort and support, these changes can become the triggers that move you towards your self-destructive behaviors in later adulthood or make it seem impossible to stop doing the ones you've already been using for years.

Some of these developmental challenges can include: becoming an empty nester; losing a job or being passed over for a promotion; unhappiness in your career or working in a toxic workplace. If you are a mental health professional or first responder, you are vulnerable to secondary traumatization and burn-out. You may have stress from an unhappy marriage, a complicated divorce or re-marriage. You might be traumatized by domestic violence. You may feel challenged by parenting your stepchildren or older children who are struggling in some way. Perhaps you have to deal with your aging or ill parents or you've been traumatized by a medical diagnosis or the onset of physical problems. Changes in finances, dealing with foreclosure, bankruptcy, or unemployment can add tremendous stress. Dealing with a partner's mental health, addictive behaviors or their medical issues can be overwhelming. Additional stressors such as being the victim of crime or a natural disaster, dealing with a loved one who is in jail, your retirement or your spouse's, illness or death of a close friend or family member can create tipping points in your life as well.

All of these things can be associated with a loss of identity, power, and control. Life transitions can feel overwhelming and scary, even more so if you associate "change" with bad outcomes or being unsafe. A prior history of losses makes the predictable losses of older adulthood more triggering. You need and deserve an external network of support to normalize your feelings, point you towards helpful resources, provide comforting and reassuring words, advocate for you, or even walk beside you to help you through the experience. If these things are not available to you, or you feel unable to take full advantage of them when they are offered, then turning to self-destructive behaviors to self-soothe, distract from fear, or re-claim a sense of control becomes an option.

Sixty-three-year-old June illustrates the negative impact that later life transitions can have, especially when you are going through them alone:

> I always took great pride in being a good mother. Now my sons are grown, living separate lives in other parts of the country. I feel such a loss of identity. My husband is and always has been a "workaholic," and is never around to do things with me. I didn't mind it so much when the boys were growing up, but now I feel so alone. It doesn't help that I have the added pressure of dealing with my Mom who is suffering from dementia. I just started

feeling more and more helpless and sad about my life situation. I never drank much as a younger person, but for the past year, it feels like getting drunk is the only way to sleep and not think about what's happening to me. But now my drinking is causing fights with my husband, so that's made things worse between us. How sad is it that my new best friend is a bottle of red wine?

When life throws you a painful curve it makes sense that the need for soothing dramatically increases. The sooner you can reach out to people in your life who are safe and trusting, even if it is humbling or makes you vulnerable to do so, the less likely it is that you will fall prey to strategies that may work in the short term, but actually create more problems and pain for you in the long term.

DRAWING EXERCISE: EXPLORING ADULT STRESSORS

A) If you are an adult, in the space below, using line, shape and color—either in concrete images or just "scribbling"—see if you can draw something that represents the adult stressors you currently experience, or have experienced in the past.

B) Now in the space below, using line, shape and color—either in concrete images or just "scribbling"—see if you can draw something that can shift the image so you can bring some soothing or hope to the picture.

6

HOW TRAUMA CAN LEAD TO SELF-DESTRUCTIVE BEHAVIORS

This part of the workbook looks at the role that past or present trauma, abuse, or neglect plays in your decision to use self-destructive acts. You may already know that you are a survivor of these painful experiences, in which case, this chapter will speak to you in a personal and meaningful way. It is also possible that you either don't remember being victimized, or you may feel strongly that you never experienced these things in your childhood or adult life. I still invite you to keep reading. As I said before, people often downplay past experiences, thinking they weren't traumatic. It's possible that reading this section will give you a new perspective about what you've gone through, which although painful, will allow more things to fall into place for you. This chapter includes wise insights from other people who have struggled with self-destructive behaviors, as well as a few writing exercises to help you gain more understanding about your thoughts, feelings, and experiences. As you read this chapter, if you are still certain that trauma, abuse, or neglect are not a part of your life, give yourself permission to move on to the next section in this workbook.

You should know that most well trained therapists consider it a great privilege to work with survivors of trauma. Their ability to be resilient, courageous, creative, loyal, and accomplished in the face of devastating life experiences is inspiring. What is interesting is the difference between the way a therapist sees you and how you may see yourself: inadequate, damaged, weak, helpless, and hopeless.

Over the years I have noticed that my view of clients who have been abused is so different from their sense of self. An unresolved traumatic past often creates distorted and confused thoughts, overwhelming negative feelings, and profoundly compromised self-esteem. Yet, ironically, like so many of my clients, you may not consciously connect your poor self-image to your trauma or painful past experiences.

As I mentioned earlier, if I asked why you have symptoms or struggle in the world, your response might be because "I'm crazy" or "I'm abnormal." A lot of trauma survivors believe they are flawed, bad, and incompetent. They may have gotten those messages from abusive or neglectful parents who made them feel responsible for the chaos and other problems that were happening at home. It stands to reason that when people you love give you critical messages over and over, they become "truths" for you, and you take them at face value. Children don't challenge the messages that come from a trusted caretaker. When you blame yourself, you don't see the role that a dysfunctional family-of-origin or a traumatic childhood can play in your thoughts, feelings, and behaviors. Instead, you may hold yourself solely responsible for the way you are in the world, believing you have problems because there is something fundamentally wrong with you.

As a result, who you are, how you interact with others, the many ways in which you get triggered, your destructive coping strategies, mood swings, and poor behavioral choices won't make sense to you. Every "symptom" gets connected to a core belief that says, "There is something defective about me." This inability to connect your struggles to your traumatic or painful past (or current situation) or to recognize the consequences of neglect or abuse adds to your distorted sense of self. Even though this is painful, you do need some way to make sense out of your issues and struggles. When there are no clear answers you probably want to fill in the blanks, and the safest and easiest target is the "flawed self."

Take a moment and consider the idea that you have been holding yourself responsible for things that have happened in the past, and these experiences may not be your fault at all. Consider the possibility that you blamed yourself because you were taught to, or because the grown-ups who actually were responsible didn't take responsibility, so the burden fell on you. If this might apply to you, in the writing exercise below, see if you can list three self-blaming thoughts that you have held onto over the years. Then give yourself permission to entertain the possibility that you weren't responsible by considering where the thought really came from: how you came to think it, or who might have taught it to you. When you've finished be sure to take some time to breathe and allow the insights to settle. Remember to put aside time for healthy self-soothing such as taking a warm bath, listening to comforting music, giving yourself a hand massage with great smelling lotion, or reading a book of positive affirmations. Or you can stand, walk around, do a crossword puzzle, or fold laundry just to re-ground and re-connect with the present.

JOURNAL EXERCISE: EXPLORING SELF-BLAME

1A) Identify a self-blaming thought (such as "I am responsible for my abuse"):

_____

_____

_____

1B) If the thought wasn't originally mine, where or how did I learn to think it?:

_____

_____

_____

2A) Identify a self-blaming thought:

_____

_____

_____

2B) If the thought wasn't originally mine, where or how did I learn to think it?:

_____

_____

_____

3A) Identify a self-blaming thought:

_____

_____

_____

3B) If the thought wasn't originally mine, where or how did I learn to think it?:

_____

_____

_____

When you come into therapy or begin to explore your issues on your own, it's as if you are carrying a large box filled with individual jigsaw puzzle pieces. If you've ever done a puzzle you know the completed picture is on the lid of the box. So, you know ahead of time what the final product will look like once the pieces are put together. As you move forward in your work you may feel as if there is a box with many different shaped pieces, but no lid: you don't know the "whole picture" ahead of time. It takes a lot of courage and a big leap of faith to keep trying to fit pieces together, especially when you don't yet recognize what the images on each individual piece even mean.

One of the reasons why you may not initially think about your experiences as traumatic or your caretakers as abusive or neglectful is the need to maintain a sense of loyalty and connection to your family. No one wants to lose that connection. Therefore, a logical coping strategy is to downplay, make excuses, or deny the fact that traumatic things actually happened.

Fifty-year-old Shawna, a recovering alcoholic, illustrates this in a therapy session:

> Where I come from, you didn't bad mouth your family members. Everything had to look good, especially to the outside world. If you wanted even a little bit of acceptance, you didn't rock the boat. Throughout my childhood, and even as an adult, I wanted my alcoholic mother to love me and approve of me. That meant ignoring all the things she did to hurt me. It also meant not getting angry at my father for never protecting me when my mother hurt me. I told myself I was getting hurt because I did something wrong. I made the abuse my fault.

When faced with the choice between "being crazy" or accepting the painful reality that you may have had abusive parents, it feels easier to choose "crazy"!

Thirty-eight-year-old Dora was terribly abused by several family members and has struggled with cutting and eating disordered behaviors for most of her life. She describes this dilemma in her therapy:

> I hate it when we talk about my family as "dysfunctional" or "abusive." Think about what you are asking me to accept—that my parents didn't love me, care about me, or protect me. If I have to choose between "being abused" or "being sick and crazy," it's less painful to see myself as nuts than to imagine my parents as evil.

As you explore your past or present relationships and experiences you may catch yourself describing abuse stories without any real emotion: sort of like you are talking about the weather. You might add disclaimers that downplay things such as, "It wasn't so bad," "I probably deserved it anyway," "I know my parents did the best they could," "It didn't have any negative effect on me," or, "That was a long time ago and it can't be affecting my life now."

You might believe that revisiting "old" feelings and thoughts will keep you stuck or are irrelevant to your current situation.

Thirty-two-year-old Jim, a very successful business owner who struggles with a sexual addiction, expresses this belief whenever therapy begins to focus on his childhood:

> Why would I want to talk about growing up on the West Coast with parents who were compulsive gamblers? The days of not having enough to eat and moving from house to house and school to school are dead and buried. Today, I can afford whatever I want. I don't want to go back there in my mind. It's depressing. And anyway, who says living with parents who gamble is "abusive?" I know kids who had it a whole lot worse than I did! Besides, it has nothing to do with my life now. The difficulties I'm having in my marriage won't be fixed by going back to the past.

Take a moment and think about the way you have described past experiences that were very painful or abusive. Notice if you have downplayed them to avoid feeling upset, or as a way to protect the people who hurt you. Perhaps you blamed yourself for what happened, or ridiculed yourself for the way in which you handled it. Maybe you've always focused on "what you did wrong." If this relates to you, in the following exercise you have the opportunity to identify the typical way you talk about these experiences, and then you'll have the chance to think about them a little differently. In other words, consider writing about the event without self-blame or self-criticism. Focus on what you did right. Just write simple statements that identify the event, rather than going into a lot of detail at this time. This approach will prevent you from becoming overwhelmed. Know that you will have many opportunities to explore any of these events more deeply in future writing and drawing exercises. Again, take time, afterwards, to breathe, re-group, and comfort yourself.

JOURNAL EXERCISE: RE-THINKING THE WAY I DESCRIBE PAINFUL EXPERIENCES

1A) I would typically describe a painful event in the following way:

_____

_____

_____

1B) A different way to describe that same event would be:

_____

_____

_____

2A) I would typically describe a painful event in the following way:

_____

_____

_____

2B) A different way to describe that same event would be:

_____

_____

_____

3A) I would typically describe a painful event in the following way:

_____

_____

_____

3B) A different way to describe that same event would be:

_____

_____

_____

It is normal for you to feel, at times, that you "don't want to go back there," believing, instead, that forgetting the past is the best way to be healed. See if the following idea makes sense to you. It's as if the painful experience was represented by your injured left arm and you go through life saying, "If I could just cut off this damaged left arm and get rid of that part of me then I would be whole again." Ironically, "getting rid" of this critical part of your life experience can never make you feel whole, just like a human body without a left arm can never be whole! It is only through the process of *accepting, embracing, and healing* that hurting and painful left arm that you can achieve genuine wholeness. Therefore, much of the therapy journey and your own work is about re-connecting with earlier, painful experiences in a way that promotes healing rather than self-blame or shame.

When you ignore, mock, or dismiss your traumatic past experiences, you deny yourself critical information that can actually help you make sense out of who you are, and why you think, feel, and behave in the ways that you do. "Connecting the dots" between past abuse or "pain narratives" and your current struggles takes a lot of courage, and, ultimately, it can set you free! Everything about you makes sense given where you've come from. And unless you can identify and address where you've come from, what has happened to you, and the impact it's had—nothing about you makes sense.

You may have distorted beliefs such as thinking you could have done something to stop your abuse, or that you should have protected someone else who was harmed in your family. You might struggle with feelings of depression and anxiety. You might have difficulty with intimacy, confusion about relationships, or a need for drama and crisis in your life. You might feel the need to self-medicate, or use destructive "coping strategies." Perhaps you have chronic body pain, negative self-image, struggle to feel "normal" in the world, or always wait for the other shoe to drop. All of those issues make sense when you are able to see yourself through the lens of past traumatic or difficult experiences.

People who are raised in emotionally unhealthy families are more likely to be impulsive, and that can play out through self-harm, substance abuse, and unhealthy adolescent and adult relationships. Many researchers in the field of trauma treatment have identified the connection between sexual, physical, emotional, verbal, and psychological abuse and neglect in childhood and adolescence, and a wide variety of self-destructive behaviors. These behaviors are used to numb, self-soothe, and distract away from painful memories. We know that children who grow up in families where the adults engage in poor communication skills such as yelling, blaming, verbal abuse, "the silent treatment," or putting kids in the middle, struggle with self-worth, feel overwhelmed with shame, and don't learn how to express their feelings or needs later in life.

All relationships are defined by boundaries: invisible lines that give us a sense of closeness to or distance from one another. In dysfunctional families the boundaries between people are either "disengaged" or far apart, so children are left feeling neglected and invisible, or they are "enmeshed," or inseparable, and children feel suffocated, lacking in privacy or violated. When you add in parents with undiagnosed and untreated substance abuse, anxiety, depression, domestic violence issues, or their own prior trauma, the odds are greatly increased that children are left with emotionally unavailable or anxious parents who cannot provide healthy role modeling, protection, guidance, consistent or predictable nurturing, or attachment. These are the parents who cannot manage their own emotional states so they can't model or provide self-soothing for their children.

Growing up with unhealthy family interactions made it hard enough for you to get by in the world. This is heightened by the fact that you may view yourself as "damaged" or "bad." But consider the additional feelings of confusion and shame when you are engaging in self-harming behaviors. In your mind, this can "up the ante," and provides even stronger evidence for your self-diagnosed "craziness." You may spend a lot of energy attempting to hide the behavior from others. The shame you feel may prevent you from being in intimate relationships, which only makes you feel more isolated. You have been through a lot. Yet, you are still standing! This is the hope we will lean on as you continue on your road to recovery!

7

MOVING AWAY FROM THE DIAGNOSIS OF "I'M CRAZY"

The Strengths-Based Approach

It's possible that you have tried a variety of strategies in an attempt to reduce or change your self-destructive behaviors. When those strategies don't work in the long term it can leave you feeling like a "failure," or cause you to lose faith in the possibility of real change happening. When you get stuck in this mindset and see yourself through a "defective" lens, you might assume that others will view you in a similar way. You might put a lot of emphasis on what is "wrong with you," including the fact that you self-harm, and present yourself to others in ways that actually support this unfair picture of who you are and what you can accomplish. You might not realize you do this, but putting yourself down or carrying your body in a "closed" posture does give off negative messages about your sense of self-worth.

As you begin to look at your self-destructive behaviors, the best and most effective approach is a strengths-based one. This encourages you to view yourself in positive ways and to focus on what is "right" about you. It means re-defining your "symptoms" as necessary coping strategies that are the common results of trauma, abuse, or chronic emotional pain. There are four major principles that go along with the strengths-based approach: normalizing, universalizing, de-pathologizing, and re-framing.

Keep in mind that the confusing thoughts, feelings, and behavioral choices related to self-destructive acts can increase your sense of feeling "weird" or "different" and add layers of guilt and shame. As previously stated, one of the most valuable things for you to hold on to is the idea that everything about you makes sense *given what you've experienced and where you've come from.* When you can connect your emotions and behaviors to past trauma or overwhelming past or present stress, the pieces begin to fit together, and your "symptoms" will start to make more sense to you.

Thirty-two-year-old Marci shows us the value of this mindset when she says:

> Out of all the things I've learned in treatment, by far the most valuable and comforting is the idea that who I am and what I struggle with actually makes sense given my family background and the things I've been through. Whenever I start to panic about my thoughts, feelings or behaviors, I remind myself that I'm not crazy—that it all makes sense—and this always seems to calm me down.

Many of the "symptoms" that you struggle with have their roots in a desire to have a witness for your story, to zone out from painful feelings, or to self-soothe. It is completely normal and healthy to want to avoid pain and find a way to express your life experiences. Sadly, the ways in which you attempt to achieve these outcomes are often harmful to your self-esteem and destructive to your mind and body. Yet it may be all you know and the only thing that has been modeled for you. Choosing to engage in self-destructive behaviors may be a way to re-create prior abuse or pain, and sometimes confirms that self-care wasn't reinforced or available to you in childhood. You're not making harmful choices because there is something wrong with you. You make harmful choices because no one ever showed you how to make good choices or made you feel worthy of good choices. *True healing can begin when you learn to separate who you are from what happened to you.*

Although every person who engages in self-destructive behavior has a unique life story, the sad truth is that countless people have experienced some form of sexual, physical, emotional, verbal, or psychological abuse, or neglect. Despite this reality, many survivors feel completely alone in their trauma experiences. Letting you know that you are not alone is a way to help you feel re-connected to others and the world at large. The feeling of being uniquely and negatively different, and therefore disconnected from others and misunderstood, can begin to go away when you learn that you are not alone in your suffering.

Stan is a 62-year-old who was emotionally neglected by his family. For most of his life he coped by drinking. He didn't seek out treatment until he was much older:

> Until I started talking to you about my life and the pain I experienced growing up, I didn't realize that other people felt the way I did. I always thought I was different, and I never wanted anyone to know about my past. I was embarrassed and ashamed of my family. I thought everyone else had great parents. I also didn't realize that I was drinking to numb out my pain—and that I'm not the only one who does that, either.

It is equally important to know that when human beings are faced with dangerous or life threatening experiences, the natural and universal desire is to want to reach out to other people for comfort and support. That is a part of our "wiring" as a person. Unfortunately, sometimes the people we want to reach to for safety are the very same people who are hurting us. This is the case if your abuser is also your caretaker. Or it may be that while one of your caretakers is abusive the other is unable or unwilling to protect you, acting like a "non-protective bystander." If no one is available to help you and you can't reach out, you will go to the next possible "survival" response—which is called "fight or flight."

Although your body wants you to "do something" when it gets threatened, oftentimes, fighting back or physically escaping is either impossible or unsafe. Typically, the perpetrator is much bigger and stronger than you. Sometimes, the abuser has a weapon, or even when they don't, they use threatening words that make you too afraid to fight back. And in some cases, children don't do fight or flight because they are so emotionally neglected that *any* attention that is paid to them, even when it's abusive, still feels better than being invisible and forgotten. So, the last "survival option" that is available is the "freeze" response. Many survivors, especially those who were abused in childhood, rely most heavily on the freeze or "dissociative" response. This could mean holding very still, not breathing, pretending to be asleep, physically collapsing, staying silent, or "giving in and acting cooperative" to avoid being hurt more. If you did that you also could have mentally escaped or "gone away" in your mind, as a way to not really be in the moment and lessen the physical and emotional pain of what was happening to you. It is a brilliant strategy to mentally escape when you can't physically escape, and it's a logical and universal response. If this was your way of coping, you were creative and smart. Unfortunately, you might not see it that way, and you might be hard on yourself or blame yourself for "not doing enough" in response to threat.

Many people who witness someone else being hurt will also resort to the "freeze" state out of terror, hopelessness, powerlessness, or in response to threats from the abuser. In these cases, "freezing" is a common and necessary survival strategy, but can leave you feeling especially guilty. This can be rooted in "survivor guilt" or feeling badly about being spared the abuse. You can also feel guilty if you think you should have somehow protected or saved the other person. Know that the way in which you coped and survived was necessary and involuntary; your body and mind did whatever it needed to do to keep you alive. And it's not reasonable to think that you actually could have saved someone else.

The tricky and complicated thing about these necessary childhood freeze responses is that they become your go-to strategy throughout life and can lead to new struggles, including, ironically, a state of helplessness and a loss of real power and control. This is because the freeze response makes you like a "deer in the headlights," and keeps you trapped and stuck. The idea that *the survival skills that once saved you in childhood are the same ones that can keep you helpless and victimized in adulthood* may be a hard concept to initially understand. The idea of letting go of a strategy like dissociation might not make sense to you at first. Therefore, your confusion, initial resistance, or uncertainty about letting go of your "zoning out" makes sense and can feel very scary!

Another useful thing to know is that when you haven't worked out traumatic experiences they leave behind real and often upsetting thoughts, body sensations, and emotions. Although it is certainly true that 10 people can experience the same trauma and respond in 10 different ways, it is equally true that people who have been traumatized can think, feel, and behave in very similar ways. If you do struggle with uncomfortable thoughts, overwhelming feelings, and body pain or discomfort, know that you are not alone and that your experiences are real and worthy of attention.

Hopefully, you are beginning to get the message that you are not "sick" because you self-harm. Holding on to this idea goes a long way towards reducing guilt and shame. When you mistakenly believe your issues and symptoms are proof that there is something wrong with you, it can leave you thinking, "I'm bad," or "the abuse was my fault." Instead, consider that "something bad happened to you," or "the abuse was the fault and responsibility of the person who chose to hurt you."

As we explore this idea of focusing on "what's right about you," this next writing and visualization exercise, adapted from Babette Rothschild, is an opportunity for you to begin to think about and identify your strengths. For some people it is easier to rattle off the things they don't like about themselves than to name the things they do like or admire. This two-part assignment will help ease you into the mindset of thinking positive thoughts. Don't worry if the exercise is hard to do, or if you can't complete it at this time. You can always re-visit it later on, and you will probably be pleasantly surprised that over time it will get easier to focus on your strengths!

VISUALIZATION AND WRITING EXERCISE: STRENGTHS THAT A LOVING RESOURCE WOULD IDENTIFY

Take a moment and think about someone currently in your life, or someone from your past, who genuinely loves and cares about you (a teacher, therapist, Rabbi, friend's parent, image of a "higher power," favorite pet). This can be anyone, living or not, related to you or not, who believes in you and has warm feelings towards you. Allow yourself to see this person or resource in your mind's eye, and imagine they are sitting next to you. Notice how they look and imagine the sound of their voice. Notice what you feel emotionally and on your body when you allow yourself to bring this resource into your thoughts. If visualizing feels challenging for you, you can use a photograph or an object that represents that person or image. Now ask that resource to list five of your strengths. Listen to the responses inside of you and write them down in the spaces provided.

FIVE OF MY STRENGTHS IDENTIFIED BY A LOVING RESOURCE

1) _____

2) _____

3) _____

4) _____

5) _____

Sit for a moment and take in that experience. Now see if you can focus on your own thoughts and feelings and write down five strengths that YOU would identify (it's ok if you identify some of the same ones!)

FIVE OF MY STRENGTHS IDENTIFIED BY ME

1) _____

2) _____

3) _____

4) _____

5) _____

Remember, whatever you wrote is fine, and you can come back to this whenever you choose. In fact, you can keep a running record of your strengths on a daily basis. The more you do it, the easier it gets!

Another concept that is an important part of the treatment of trauma and self-destructive behaviors is "re-framing." Re-framing doesn't change the reality of an experience. It does, however, let you think and feel differently about that experience. And the good news is, when you can change your beliefs about past abuse, how you feel about your body, why a trusted caretaker mistreated you, or why you went through a painful life stressor, the impact of those experiences changes as well. This can be a tremendous relief if up until now you believed that you couldn't stop your destructive acts unless something externally changed first.

Forty-year-old Mindy experienced a childhood of terrible sexual and emotional abuse. She had tried, repeatedly, to get her father to take responsibility for abusing her. Early in therapy she said:

> I've been abusing my body in many ways for years. I always believed that until my father admitted what he did to me, and understood the impact that it had on me, I would have to keep hurting myself and I would forever be depressed. I'm starting to realize that if I keep waiting for him to "get it" or apologize, then I'm still giving him power and control over my life. Maybe I can get better and stop hurting my body even if my father doesn't cooperate.

One of the most important re-frames is the idea that the person who hurt you doesn't need to apologize, cooperate in therapy, own their behavior, express guilt about what they've done or even feel compassion towards you in order for you to heal or let go of your self-destructive acts. All that matters is *your* ability to think and feel differently about your experiences: letting go of thoughts that leave you feeling responsible or "damaged." All destructive behaviors can be stopped when you are able to see what was done to you through a more accurate and compassionate lens.

8

CONNECTING TO OTHERS AND MANAGING YOUR EMOTIONS

One of the things that will really help you work through your self-destructive behaviors is to understand the role of attachment and its impact on your ability to handle your emotional states. Seeking out and maintaining safe, healthy attachment is a universal need, and a part of our biology as human beings. Attaching to people you love lets you feel protected, safe, physically comforted and soothed, and connected to others.

When you come into the world your first task is to successfully attach to the primary people who are taking care of you. You have to attach in order to survive because you are completely helpless and dependent! If your family is loving, pre-dictable, safe, and emotionally available, then attaching is easy to do. As an infant you were born with a very limited number of resources for self-soothing. You had a sucking reflex, you could look away when something startled or upset you, and you could "zone out" or dissociate to tune out experiences that distressed your fragile system. Everything else that you learned to do was supposed to come from the soothing you got from your caretakers.

When you were upset as an infant you cried as a way to reach out to others, and you were appropriately communicating your desire for physical and emotional comfort and connection. If you were spoken to in a soothing singsong voice, rocked, stroked, and gazed at lovingly, your body relaxed and you felt comforted and calm. If your caretakers responded in these loving and soothing ways they were supporting your legitimate needs and teaching you to trust in the fact that others would be available to you when you needed them.

Therefore, the attachment pattern that got established for you was crucial, since it directly connected to your future ability to self-soothe and to manage your emotional states. If there was secure attachment, you looked for soothing and learned to trust that you would get what you needed. If you consistently received comfort, in time, you mastered the ability to use your own internal resources for self-soothing when your caretakers were temporarily unavailable. Over time, the positive "learned" experiences of comforting got imprinted on your body and you began to regulate yourself in ways that mirrored what your loving caretakers were doing. If you were allowed to develop healthy ways to self-soothe, it means that as you faced the future stressors of adolescence and adulthood you would be able to cope effectively and not feel the need to turn to unhealthy strategies such as cutting, bingeing, or drinking.

But if you *do* rely on these behaviors to cope and self-soothe, there is the possibility that you didn't get the consistent, secure attachment and comforting responses you needed and deserved. This was not your fault. You had no control over emotionally unavailable caretakers who may have entered into parenthood with their own unresolved trauma, addictions, significant mental illness, a chronic medical condition, intense family stressors, undiagnosed and untreated anxiety or depression. Sadly, many primary caretakers are emotionally unavailable or easily triggered by a child's need for close attachment. In these situations, when the child cries out for comfort, the caretakers will go into a fight/flight or freeze response because they are threatened or overwhelmed by the sound of crying. This means the infant's need for soothing will instead be met with parental aggression, avoidance, withdrawal, or spacing out.

If your caretakers were unavailable, inconsistent, abusive, easily triggered, dysfunctional, or violent, then your necessary task of attaching was complicated and compromised. You may have attempted to use crying, charming smiles, reaching out gestures, cooing and making other sounds to engage your disinterested or unresponsive caretakers. *Their lack of response was not because you were unlovable or undeserving.*

You may have gotten the message that you were "emotionally needy," "high maintenance," "overly sensitive," "demanding," or "selfish." The reality is parents often give children these labels when *they* are unable to meet a child's legitimate emotional needs. It's a way for parents to take the focus off of their own shortcomings. They put the blame on the child instead. But it is the *adult's* obligation and responsibility to create a secure attachment, not the child's. If your caretaker was neglectful, abusive, or non-protective, the impact was the same: you felt unworthy of love and attention. Over time, this repeated "childhood propaganda," or untrue message, becomes accepted by you as a core truth. It may be one of the reasons why you stopped showing emotions and lost the ability to effectively communicate your needs to others. It also deprived you of the ability to learn how to do self-protection and self-care.

As you explore the possible connection between using self-destructive behaviors to manage overwhelming feelings and not having secure attachments in childhood, take a moment to revisit memories of how your caretakers responded when you were emotionally upset. In the journal exercise below, answer the questions from whatever memories you have, along with whatever information you've been given from siblings and other relatives about the caretaking you received growing up. You can focus on your caretaker's words, expressed feelings, body language, and behavioral responses. The purpose of this is not to keep blaming your parents. Rather, it is to help you make sense out of why you still find it hard to manage your different emotions. When you answer these questions, know that whatever thoughts or feelings come up for you are normal and okay. Take the time you need to either breathe and re-group after finishing the statements, or to stop mid-way through if you start to feel too uncomfortable. Remember to refer back to the earlier suggestions about self-soothing and re-grounding.

JOURNAL EXERCISE: EXPLORING CARETAKER RESPONSES TO YOUR EMOTIONAL NEEDS

1) When I felt angry as a child, the typical response from my caretakers was:

_____

_____

_____

2) If I became sad and started to cry, the typical response from my caretakers was:

_____

_____

_____

3) If I needed encouragement or support for something that was challenging in my life, the typical response from my caretakers was:

_____

_____

_____

4) When I was frightened and needed reassurance about my safety or wellbeing, the typical response from my caretakers was:

_____

_____

_____

5) If I physically got hurt, the typical response from my caretakers was:

_____

_____

_____

6) If I made a mistake of any kind, the typical response from my caretakers was:

_____

_____

_____

Take a few moments and let your answers sink in. This may be the first time you've considered a possible connection between your caretakers' responses to your physical, emotional, and psychological needs and the extent to which you do or don't know how to engage in consistent self-care. If you grew up in a dysfunctional family, it is likely that legitimate emotional and physical needs continued to be downplayed or ignored, and you learned to feel a sense of shame for wanting anything. Even if your caretakers were not directly abusive, you might have been traumatized if they acted like non-protective bystanders. This means that although they did not directly harm you, their inability or unwillingness to shield you or get you away from someone harmful became a form of abuse and caretaker betrayal in and of itself.

Even as you continued to grow up, you needed to find ways to attach to unavailable caretakers. It was probably impossible for you to think of your parents as toxic, unloving, or bad: that reality would make it too difficult to attach and bond with them. Instead, you could unconsciously "make sense" out of your parents' neglectful or abusive actions by taking ownership of the poor parenting, telling yourself you were not loved because there was something wrong with *you*. When you tell yourself "my parent isn't bad, I am bad," you can still successfully attach to that parent. Although this may have been necessary to believe at the time, self-blame may be at the core of the negative thoughts that haunt you and, in your mind, make it okay to use self-punishing behaviors.

Attachment patterns can be complicated in families. Obviously, the ideal kind of attachment is a "secure" one: caretakers are consistent, reliable, willing and able to bond, protect, and nurture. Other styles of attachment can be confusing. Sometimes a caretaker is available and responds appropriately and at other times their response to the same situation is totally inappropriate. Oftentimes, the people who are supposed to be the most supportive are the ones who are the scariest or they, themselves, are frightened and become helpless. Keep in mind that you can only learn what you witness and experience. So a lack of secure attachment and comfort will profoundly affect whether or not you develop your own tools for soothing later in life.

In addition, if you were in survival mode, you took on the behaviors, body postures, and movements that were most adaptive in your family. This means you acted, moved, and spoke in ways that kept you safe and were considered "acceptable" by caretakers. Often this manifests in collapsed or closed off posture, avoiding direct eye contact with others, and using a voice that is passive, not assertive. Although these responses kept you safe, you couldn't gain mastery over healthier ways to communicate or advocate for yourself. Your body language communicated a shamed self, and gave others information about how you expected to be treated in relationships. In the long term, this can create a tragic self-fulfilling prophecy, as predators seem to have radar for sensing more vulnerable children and adults, and are able to exploit and re-victimize them without consequences.

As you read this, keep in mind that most people do not come into the therapy process or approach this work with an awareness of how early childhood attachment and relationship dynamics profoundly impact current behaviors and a core sense of self. These are realizations that unfold, in time, with the help of a trained professional.

Fifty-year-old Brian spent much of his childhood in foster care and was repeatedly abused and neglected. Early in treatment he said:

> Ok, I get that I had a really horrible childhood, and I even understand that I have the right to be angry about it. But that doesn't explain my addiction to porn and why I keep winding up with women who hurt me and cheat on me. I feel like despite my childhood, I am responsible for the mess I am making of my adult life. Now there's no one to blame but myself.

Despite the sad reality of the impact of insecure and disorganized attachments, the exciting news is that when you are able to reach out to other people and accept the safe attempts they make to connect with you (including with a healthy partner, close friend, or therapist) it can help to repair those earlier attachment losses. As you continue to find the courage to reach out and the curiosity to pursue safe and trusting relationships, you will also be able to begin experimenting with healthier self-soothing strategies. Learning how to trust other people allows you to tap into your own inner wisdom and that's when true healing can begin!

9

WHAT SELF-DESTRUCTIVE BEHAVIORS REALLY MEAN

Hopefully, you now have a better understanding of the role that the developmental challenges of adolescence and later adulthood, difficulties managing emotions, unhealthy family relationships, and attachment wounds can play in self-destructive behaviors. The next part of the puzzle involves an understanding of the ways in which self-destructive behaviors communicate, re-enact, and attempt to re-story or re-write prior traumatic experiences and pain narratives.

Self-destructive behavior is often a non-verbal way to "communicate" to other people deeper information about your thoughts, feelings, needs, and experiences. This may be a brand new concept for you. We all communicate without words: through body language, facial expressions, tone, pitch, and speed of voice, the expression in our eyes, or the avoidance of eye contact. It's a form of communication that goes beyond words, and is often inconsistent with verbal statements. A mother can say to her child "I love you," but if at the same time she folds her arms across her chest and avoids eye contact it cancels out the verbal message and creates confusion for the child.

You may display the same inconsistency when you tell someone in your life that "nothing is wrong and you're not angry" yet you withdraw or make aggressive behavioral choices that hurt and punish your body. Another example is if you verbally claim to be comfortable with intimacy, yet continue to binge and gain weight or spend hours looking at pornography on the Internet, resulting in less sexual closeness with your partner. Without shaming yourself, take a moment to notice if there are ways in which you give off mixed messages. Gaining insight about this is important because the disconnect between what you say and what you do may be confusing or frustrating to loved ones and wind up depriving you of the support and understanding you deserve to have from them.

WRITING EXERCISE: MY VERBAL AND NON-VERBAL MESSAGES

Take some time and answer the following statements. Remember the idea is not to judge or feel shame. It's to help you gain insight, which is the first step towards change. Make sure you take some time to breathe and rest afterwards.

1) When I feel angry at someone I communicate it with words by saying:

_____

_____

_____

and I communicate it non-verbally by doing:

_____

_____

_____

2) When I feel sad I communicate it with words by saying:

_____

_____

_____

and I communicate it non-verbally by doing:

_____

_____

_____

3) When I feel overwhelmed I communicate it with words by saying:

_____

_____

_____

and I communicate it non-verbally by doing:

_____

_____

_____

4)   When I feel anxious or afraid I communicate it with words by saying:

_____

_____

_____

and I communicate it non-verbally by doing:

_____

_____

_____

5)   When I need guidance or support, I communicate it with words by saying:

_____

_____

_____

and I communicate it non-verbally by doing:

_____

_____

_____

Ironically, our non-verbal communication is a much more honest form of self-expression. We can all "manipulate" or choose words to please someone, avoid threat or conflict, or get a desired outcome. But the body doesn't lie, so most of what we express non-verbally is spontaneous, authentic, and often beyond our conscious control. When you find the courage to be curious about your non-verbal communication and the way in which your self-destructive behavior "tells a story you haven't been able to put into words," it often opens the door to a much deeper understanding of yourself.

Remember that even if you are unable or unwilling to verbally express your emotional needs or pain narratives, there is still a natural desire to share it with caring witnesses and to break the cycle of secrecy and denial. When words fail because they've been taken from you, feel useless, or just aren't there, it makes sense that you will seek out other ways to "tell" your story.

One of the ways you can be curious about your story is to be open to the idea that how and where you hurt yourself is not accidental, coincidental, or meaningless. You are using your body as a "canvas," showing the pain you cannot talk about. Eating disorders, addictions, and self-mutilation become a way for sexual, emotional, and physical abuse to be communicated. When you can "de-code" the hidden messages in your self-destructive acts your pain narrative is revealed. Be curious about the location and nature of your injuries, and why you lean towards one method over another. Think about what the addiction, eating disorder, injury, or hurt part of your body would "say" if it could talk.

As you find the courage to begin "translating" your actions and focusing on the deeper meaning, you can look at two critical things: *re-enacting* a part of the pain narrative so it can be *revealed and witnessed,* and/or *re-storying* or trying to change the ending, to *get back a sense of closure, power, or control.* Let's look at some of the more common issues associated with the re-enactment and re-storying of eating disordered behaviors, addiction, and self-mutilation. Although this will give you some ideas to consider, ultimately, what matters most are *your* interpretations.

I want to repeat the idea that some of these insights might be uncomfortable or triggering for you. What's most important is that you continue to pay attention to how you feel as you move forward with the workbook, and that you give yourself permission to slow down, take a break, or stop, before the feelings become overwhelming. Keep practicing the strategies that re-connect you to the present or bring you a sense of comfort. In addition to the ideas that have already been repeated several times, you can read ahead and learn about additional techniques that will help you manage difficult thoughts or feelings in Part IV of this workbook.

Eating Disorders

The three most common ways that people do eating disordered behaviors are bingeing, bulimia, and anorexia. If you do any of these behaviors, consider that anorexia, bulimia, and binge eating each uniquely re-enact and re-story specific aspects of abuse, trauma, or pain, and that you are choosing one behavior over another for conscious and unconscious reasons.

Binge Eating

People who binge typically describe episodes of uncontrolled eating. They eat large amounts of food quickly and often in a "zoned out" state. The food is not purged or "gotten rid of" and they don't stop until there is physical pain or exhaustion. The binges are usually done in secret and can create strong feelings of guilt and shame. When you think about connecting this behavior to the idea of "re-enacting" or re-living a past experience, consider the fact that *forcing* something into the body that is unwanted might possibly relate to some form of sexual trauma. It's worth being curious about the physical pain that bingeing creates in the body. If you do bingeing behaviors, you probably have experienced discomfort, fatigue, or pain, in your throat, tongue, jaw, neck, or stomach. You may relate to the sensation of gagging, having trouble swallowing, or feeling nauseous.

It helps to be curious about these body sensations: noticing the thoughts, words, or images that come up for you. In therapy you can explore "when else and with whom else you have experienced those thoughts and feelings." The physical pain you feel when you binge may possibly be a way to re-create a past experience of forced penetration or oral sex, or nausea in response to some other sexual violation.

Another potential re-enactment is the confused feeling you get when something that is supposed to be nurturing (food) "turns on you" and becomes a source of pain (like a caretaker who betrayed you in some way). People who binge often describe this "love–hate" relationship with food, and that same ambivalent feeling might relate to your experiences with a trusted caretaker who harmed or betrayed you in some way.

You might also consider the possibility that forcing food into the body re-enacts a total disregard for what you need and feel. If you are like most people who binge, you eat way beyond the point of actually feeling hungry. You ignore the signs your body gives you and continue to force yourself to eat. If an abuser disregarded the pain or terror they were creating and continued to hurt you, your bingeing might be an unconscious re-enactment of something that was modeled and normalized by the perpetrator.

When you binge, you might sometimes be in a numb or dissociative state. This means standing outside of yourself, watching, and not actually tasting what you are eating. Dissociation is often used to cope with and survive sexual trauma, and your uncontrolled eating may be a way to re-enact that part of your trauma story: zoning out as a way to feel safer in the world.

Lastly, it's important to realize that bingeing is about keeping a secret, and often one that you feel ashamed of, and your eating behavior may be a way to re-live those prior experiences as well. It re-enacts the idea that something major is happening in your life and it is something you cannot fully control. Yet you aren't able to share it with anyone around you. It is a burden to keep the secret of being sexually abused, just as it can be a burden to keep the secret of hiding food and bingeing.

Another trauma that can be "re-lived" through bingeing is the family experience of "emotional incest." If you relate to this, you may have been forced to be a parent's "emotional partner." This means you were expected to provide your parent with reassurance, a listening ear, companionship, and the comfort that should have been supplied by their adult partner. In this situation, the boundaries are inappropriate and you are made to feel guilty for and discouraged from wanting appropriate amounts of space and privacy. Stuffing too much food into your body can be a way to "show" this unhealthy family dynamic of feeling "suffocated" and having no boundaries.

If you binge, there are several possible ways in which that behavior is an attempt to change the ending of an upsetting experience for you or a way to *re-story it*. This certainly plays out in cases of sexual trauma. If you are like many sexual abuse survivors, you either hold yourself responsible for the abuse, believe you could have or should have done something to stop it, or worse, think you liked it or "participated" in it because your body responded. Oftentimes, an abuser deliberately gives you pleasure or brings you to orgasm as a way to trick you into believing "you wanted it to happen." In your confused state, it also decreases the likelihood that you will tell anyone about the abuse. If you have this distorted sense of being sexually molested, and feel angry at yourself, bingeing can feel like a "logical" and necessary way to punish your body.

Another common experience is using bingeing as a way to re-claim body control. The extra weight gain can make you feel powerful as you literally take up more space. In your mind it also creates a "shield of protection" around you, making your body look and feel "less sexual," and reducing the possibility that you will be sexually attractive to others. If sexual touch triggers you by putting you into a flashback during sex (giving you images and feelings that relate to a prior frightening sexual experience), and you don't know how to bring yourself back into the present, then becoming less desirable to your partner becomes a creative way to avoid sex and the accompanying overwhelming experience of getting re-triggered.

For many people bingeing can be a full time job. You need time to buy the food, hide it, plan the binge and secretly engage in it. As a result, in the short term there is an isolating part to it that can increase your sense of safety. When you are so wrapped up in food you don't have any time to be with other people. In addition, food can be used to self-medicate (making you feel better by numbing out upsetting emotions) while giving you a sense of being nurtured and comforted. When you don't have healthy resources to manage your emotions this can feel like a way to get those needs met.

It is also worth exploring the possibility that bingeing can help you cut short a dissociative state. Feeling pain or exhaustion after overeating can re-connect you to your body, helping you feel alive and present, and this can increase your sense of control. In your most honest moments, you might agree that food feels like a "safe and trusted friend." You know the effects of bingeing and like that you can count on those feelings whenever you do the behavior. This may be your most reliable "relationship," and it gives you at least one thing you can depend upon in your life. Lastly, the act of bingeing is distracting and a great way to literally swallow back down overwhelming and painful memories that bubble up unannounced whenever you get triggered. In the short term, that becomes a creative way to not deal with or face things that require great courage to address.

Bulimia

People who do bulimia quickly eat large amounts of food and continue to binge until they are exhausted or in physical pain. It's different from bingeing because then they try to get rid of the food through purging behaviors like making themselves vomit, abusing laxatives, diuretics, or enemas, or excessive exercise. They may also severely limit how much they eat in between binges. They may feel a loss of control over these behaviors and can do them several times a week or many times throughout the day.

When we look at the connection between bulimia and sexual trauma, we can see several possible examples of re-enacting and re-storying. If you do bulimic behaviors, the physical act of forcing something into the body and then getting rid of it may be symbolic for you. Like bingeing, bulimia creates physical pain and fatigue in your throat, tongue, jaw, neck, or stomach. This is made worse by the physical violence of purging behaviors that create stomach cramps, rectal pain or bleeding, or burning sensations in the throat. Again, you may be re-enacting the sensation of gagging, having trouble swallowing, feeling nauseous, or having intense diarrhea. These are the same physical symptoms that can happen when you are sexually abused.

Allow yourself to be curious about those experiences in your body and think about when else you may have felt them. Be open to the idea that the specific way you purge is not a coincidence and may relate to the part of your body that was violated and harmed during sexual trauma. Consider the possibility that sexual trauma including forced oral or anal sex may be a part of the deeper communication of the physical pain or discomfort you recreate with bulimia.

The acts of bingeing and purging can also represent "not being in control." This is a very real and constant feeling for sexual abuse survivors who were repeatedly violated. So many things are taken away from sexual abuse survivors including: their right to privacy; a feeling of innocence or safety; appropriate body boundaries; and the belief that people can be trusted. Many people who get caught up in the cycle of bingeing and purging also describe a feeling of being "out of control." They want the behaviors to stop but don't know how to make that happen.

Just as we discussed with bingeing, bulimia can be a way to show a complete disregard for your body. This is certainly what abusers model when they sexually molest their victims. In this case, the wellbeing of your body is ignored during the binge phase and then again during violent acts of purging. Allow yourself to be curious about who might have given you the message that it was acceptable to mistreat your body in such abusive ways.

As is the case with other eating disorders, feelings of secrecy and shame get repeated when you are hiding and covering up two different self-destructive acts. In addition, you may feel as if you have to lie about the behaviors to loved ones, pretending everything is ok when it's not or even denying that you are doing the behaviors at all. If you relate to this, you know there are strong feelings of guilt, confusion, and fear that go along with the secrecy. You might be terrified about "getting caught," while another part of you hopes you will be found out so you can get help. Think about all of those feelings and notice if they have any possible connection to a past experience of sexual trauma.

Lastly, consider the possibility that if you purge by making yourself vomit, it may be a re-enactment of either wanting to or actually vomiting after a sexual violation. It is very common for a victim of sexual trauma to feel "sick to their stomach" before, during, or after they are harmed. If the perpetrator was drunk, it is even possible that you had to clean up their vomit.

Bulimia also replays the double-edged sword of something that is nurturing (food) "turning on you," and causing you pain. The healthy, nurturing part of food morphs into a weapon that hurts you when you overeat. It takes on an additional self-harming component when you violently get rid of the food by purging. The love–hate relationship you have with food as you binge and purge may re-enact those same love–hate feelings you felt towards your perpetrator. It makes sense that food becomes a symbol representing a caretaker since both are supposed to be a source of nurturance that comforts us and helps keep us alive.

Bulimia can also be a sign of a history of physical abuse. Although it can be hard to focus on this aspect of bingeing and purging, keep in mind that these behaviors are acts of physical, violent aggression against your body. This is particularly true when you do them over and over again. This puts tremendous strain on your body, physically harming and weakening it, while creating distress and pain. Bingeing and purging take a huge medical toll, and it may somehow remind you of the pain you felt when an abuser physically hurt you.

When you add the second behavior of purging you dramatically increase your body pain. So it's possible that these behaviors speak to you because they have a degree of physical violence attached to them. Your abusers may have spent less time trying to win over your trust and "rewarding" you after hurting you, and more time using threats to guarantee that you wouldn't fight back or tell anyone about the abuse. In these cases, perpetrators tend to be more sociopathic, which means they feel no shame or guilt when they do harm. They have no empathy for their victims and have no concern about the pain their victims feel. When a sociopath abuses, he or she actually gets a sick sense of pleasure from the physical pain and distress they are causing because it makes them feel powerful.

You can also think about bulimia as a possible re-enactment of verbal, psychological, or emotional trauma. If you experienced these forms of abuse, they may have left you feeling insignificant and bad. Sadly, you may have gotten the message that your caretakers were "disgusted" with you. Interestingly enough, purging behaviors may also leave you feeling "disgusting." This emotion is worth exploring, as it may connect back to earlier experiences of being made to feel worthless. Emotional abuse or neglect can leave you feeling unloved, hopeless, helpless, and very alone in the world. Notice if any of these feelings connect with your state of mind after you binge or purge.

When we look at the possible ways in which bulimic behaviors are an attempt to change the ending or "re-story" past trauma, you may see it as a way to "cleanse or rid the body" of bad thoughts, feelings of "being dirty," or intense guilt and shame. Purging is also a way to release unspoken memories and to non-verbally express rage; getting things out without using words. You may believe you are reclaiming a sense of control over your body when you can get rid of what's been forced inside of you.

Just as we discussed with bingeing, bulimia is a way to punish your body, only it's a double whammy. You are hurting it through forced eating and then again through the violent act of purging the food. If you still feel guilty because you "should have done more" to end the abuse, think you "participated in it," felt "pleasure" while you were being molested, "felt betrayed by your body," or for any other reason, you might believe that this justifies intensely punishing your body with bulimic behaviors. Although you read this earlier, it's worth repeating: freezing or not fighting back when abused is a necessary survival strategy. You never willingly "participate" in acts of sexual trauma. Feeling aroused when the body is touched in certain ways is a normal and involuntary response. It doesn't mean you want to be violated. *And your body didn't betray you—your abuser did.*

It is also possible that the need to punish and significantly hurt your body connects to guilt because your perpetrator involved other victims and forced you to "participate" by making you do sexually inappropriate things to others. Although this is not often talked about, it is more common than you might think, and understandably leaves victims feeling completely ashamed and confused. If you relate to this, please know that forcing you to hurt another child was another way to victimize both you and that child. Given everything we have discussed about the genuine helplessness and powerlessness of victims, know that "going along with it" was really another way to survive and you truly had no choice.

If you feel "weird" and "crazy" when you purge, the behavior may be re-enacting a sense of "badness." This idea might fit with your core sense of self, and the messages you received from your abuser.

There is even greater isolation with bulimia since you spend energy engaging in two secretive, time-consuming behaviors. It may take hours to plan the binge, buy and hide the food, and then wait for the appropriate or private time to overeat. The same is true for your purging. It requires a degree of privacy and can take up hours of time. This means much of your day or evening begins to revolve around the binge–purge cycle. This takes you away from interactions with others and increases a sense of isolation and despair. Yet in your mind, that "isolation" might feel like a necessary way to be safe in the world and to decrease the likelihood of getting hurt by others.

Anorexia

Anorexia is an extremely dangerous behavior. Nearly 20 percent of people who struggle with this issue will die from it. It has the highest mortality rate of any "mental disorder." It often appears with the onset of puberty at a time when the body is undergoing significant changes. If you severely restrict your calories, this will affect your ability to maintain your body weight. People who have full-blown anorexia typically lose at least 15 percent of their total body weight. You may struggle with an intense fear of gaining weight or "becoming fat" which makes you pre-occupied with food and calories. You keep dieting even when you are already too thin, and have a distorted view of your body size and shape. You may be like many people who limit what they eat and feel anxious about foods that have fat in them. Since the hormone that is required to menstruate is stored in fat cells, completely avoiding this food group will cause you to stop menstruating which can create serious problems with fertility and bone loss later in life.

Despite the fact that anorexia can feel like a particularly challenging behavior to treat, if you are not needing to be hospitalized then focusing on the deeper meaning behind the behavior, rather than food journals, weigh-ins, and calorie counting, can actually move you forward and reduce the likelihood of relapses.

Allow yourself to explore the possibility that anorexia is connected to emotional or physical neglect or abandonment. The act of starving can be information about feeling ignored or being deprived of nurturance. You are making yourself smaller and smaller in the world, which leaves you invisible and extremely vulnerable. You don't allow yourself to take up any space. These are feelings that mirror the experiences of neglect. The denial of food is a re-enactment of a total disregard for the body and this, too, may have its roots in prior neglect and a lack of adequate nurturance.

If your starving behaviors ever became extreme enough you most likely wound up being hospitalized. Although you were probably strongly resistant to hospitalization, you might actually have been unconsciously re-enacting the loss of freedom, a sense of always being watched, an obsessive focus on your body, and the loss of body control that comes from "forced feedings." Think about a possible connection between personal losses in your life and the "loss" that comes with anorexic behavior. Staying with this idea of loss can move you to a much deeper understanding of the pain and grief you may be trying to communicate and resolve.

When you explore the possibility that anorexia is a way to re-enact aspects of sexual trauma, consider the fact that starving is a statement about the loss of body ownership. When you are significantly under-weight you may no longer connect to or feel your body. People who are sexually abused often report feeling as if their bodies no longer belong to them. Instead they become the "property" of the perpetrator.

Severely restricting calories can also re-enact a dissociative state as you begin to feel "spacey," light-headed, and dizzy when you don't eat. Starving leaves you disconnected from your body in the same way that sexual trauma can. When you are sexually abused you often have to resort to dissociation in order to survive the physical, emotional, and psychological pain of what's happening to you. This is especially true when you are trapped and cannot escape the situation. When there are no words for your sexual abuse narrative, the re-enactment of constant dissociation might be the creative way to keep alive a connection to an otherwise unspoken and terrifying experience.

Your restrictive eating might leave you feeling ashamed and forced to be quite secretive. Most people work hard to hide the fact that they are not eating. They will lie and do other deceptive behaviors to fool people into thinking that they are taking in enough calories. These misleading and dishonest behaviors don't mean you are a bad person—more likely they are re-enactments of the deceptive practices that abusers modeled or the secret-keeping they forced you to do while sexually abusing you.

Some of the re-storying dynamics of anorexia parallel the other eating disordered behaviors. It is a way to punish your body for "participating" in sexual acts, or for not being able to fight back or tell anyone about the abuse. If you mistakenly believe the trauma was your fault, then in your mind it will make sense to be punished by not giving your body the food it needs to thrive. Many people who do this behavior have feelings of rage towards their abusers, but don't feel safe or comfortable expressing that rage outwardly. Instead, they hold on to those intensely angry feelings, turning them inward. This, in turn, fuels the need to punish the body by cruelly depriving it of food.

When females lose a significant amount of weight they no longer have visible breasts, hips, and other natural curves that make the body feminine. For some people, this feels like a way to protect themselves from sexual advances. When you become too thin you are less desirable and seem too physically fragile to participate in sexual activity.

When anorexia is not about re-storying neglect, it may be a way to fight back from caretaking that feels suffocating. Depriving the body of food (something nurturing) is a way to re-story the fact that the attachment with caretakers was actually over-bearing. You may relate to this if you had alcoholic parents who couldn't hold appropriate boundaries or respect your right to privacy and space. Perhaps you had dysfunctional parents who engaged in "emotional incest" by making you their confidante or buddy, or forcing you to be their emotional spouse in the family. Withholding food psychologically feels like the opposite of the oppressive, blurred boundaries you may have experienced growing up.

Deciding what you do and don't put into your body can also be a powerful attempt to reclaim a sense of body control. If you relate to this, a loss of control may be the result of a body violation, or it may be an emotional issue related to rigid, controlling parents who expect and demand perfection, or discourage independence and privacy. People who go all day without eating can feel inaccurately "proud" of the "self-discipline" it takes, and even feel superior to others who "give in" and eat when they feel hunger pains. In their minds, not eating is being totally in control of their bodies, and that gives them back a false sense of power.

Severely limiting how much you eat can also create a feeling of euphoria or being "high." This comes, in part, from the light-headedness that happens when you don't take in enough calories. This might temporarily short-circuit your negative feelings and internal messages of self-loathing. It may feel like the only way you can briefly achieve a more positive emotional state. In addition, your preoccupation with not eating, and obsessively thinking about what you did eat, distracts you away from other trauma-based thoughts and emotions that feel too overwhelming or frightening to address.

Another way you can re-claim a sense of power and control is to use your destructive behavior to punish others, particularly family members. Starving behaviors and significant weight loss are genuinely frightening to parents and spouses. They often feel helpless and even "held hostage" by the behaviors. If you have unresolved anger towards a loved one, holding on to your scary behavior is a way to get back at them.

Ironically, the other side of that same coin is the fact that anorexia can get you tremendous attention from significant others and may be a way for you to lure them back into being more emotionally engaged and concerned. Sadly, some family members get more connected when symptoms are worse, but then disconnect again when things are better. Of course, the reinforcing message is that connection can only be maintained when you stay "symptomatic." In other cases, narcissistic parents might only show interest in their child or express approval when that child is "model thin." This can keep alive restrictive eating habits well into adulthood.

WRITING EXERCISE: EXPLORING THE DEEPER MEANING OF AN EATING DISORDER

If you have ever used eating disordered behaviors as a creative way to cope, take a few minutes to look at the possible ways in which your actions have re-enacted and/or re-storied a prior painful or traumatic experience. Remember to approach this work with non-judgmental curiosity and compassion.

Set a timer for 15 minutes. This will prevent you from getting "lost" in the exercise. At the end of 15 minutes if you need more time, re-set the timer for one more 15-minute interval. When you finish be sure to do something that feels soothing such as listening to calming music, drinking a cup of tea, or massaging your hands with scented hand lotion. It is also ok to do something that grounds you in the present, like a household chore, math problems, or wordsearch puzzles.

1) The behavior I engaged in:

_____

_____

_____

What I might have been attempting to re-enact:

_____

_____

_____

What I might have been attempting to re-story:

_____

_____

_____

2) The behavior I engaged in:

_____

_____

_____

What I might have been attempting to re-enact:

_____

_____

_____

What I might have been attempting to re-story:

_____

_____

_____

3) The behavior I engaged in:

_____

_____

_____

What I might have been attempting to re-enact:

_____

_____

_____

What I might have been attempting to re-story:

_____

_____

_____

Addictions

You can also look at the deeper meaning of your addictions. Abusing drugs, alcohol, nicotine, and other substances, compulsive gambling and shopping, and sexual addictions are all designed to make you feel better and create distractions to keep your pain from surfacing and overwhelming you. As stated earlier, it helps to be curious about why you choose your specific form of self-destructive behavior. Focusing on your addictive behaviors and noticing the thoughts, feelings, images, body sensations, and movements that come up for you becomes a way to process the deeper meanings. Again what is most important are the interpretations and insights that you come up with, but here are some possible messages that can be de-coded when dealing with these behaviors.

In many cases, the numbing you feel when doing your addictive behavior can re-enact a dissociative "state of being" that is familiar and comfortable. If you want to keep returning to a place of being "zoned out" it's worth exploring that both on your own and with the support of a trained mental health professional. It might connect to your belief that the only way to stay safe is in a "freeze" state. It might speak to earlier attachment issues, reflecting an unconscious fear that you won't know how to feel or deal with emotions because no one gave you strategies for self-soothing. Substance abuse becomes a way to keep those feelings hidden.

When you are numb, you actually lose power and control and this might be a re-enactment of "learned helplessness." When you are drunk or high, your judgment and behaviors are impaired, making it much harder for you to engage in self-care or self-protection. In essence, when you are "under the influence" you become helpless, and this might be familiar and "normal" for you if you've had prior experiences of painful things happening that were not in your control. The fact that you could not protect yourself in the past gets re-played again and again when you engage in addictive acts that continue to leave you unprotected.

You might even choose behaviors that mimic your alcoholic or drugging caretaker as a way to "connect" with them. This might be a literal way to connect in cases where a parent will only spend time with you when you are both drinking or getting high. Sometimes, imitating a caretaker's addiction gives others powerful information about your family-of-origin dynamics by "showing" them what you lived with and endured growing up. This idea can be especially hard to accept and prompts a lot of denial if you swore, in childhood, to "never be like" your substance-abusing parent.

Over time, all addictions eventually spiral out of control and this may be a re-enactment of how out of control your life felt in the past. Pretending you have it all together, and looking okay to the outside world when you really aren't, can also relate to your past experiences of having to pretend things were fine when they weren't. Many children who grow up in toxic and abusive families are implicitly taught to never acknowledge or talk about their family's problems. Secret-keeping and pretending nothing is wrong is normalized and encouraged. Consider the possibility that the denial you lived with in your family transferred into the denial about your own addiction problems.

Like eating disordered behaviors, sexual addictions and substance abuse re-enact physical neglect, a de-valuing of self, and a total disregard for the body: a core value that perpetrators promoted in your childhood. If you ever ventured into dangerous neighborhoods to score your drugs, had sexual encounters with strangers, drove drunk or high, or made other poor decisions while under the influence, this can be seen as a re-creation of the times you were put in physical or sexual danger in the past.

Like eating disordered behaviors, addictions are isolating and speak to a basic lack of attachment and fear of close connections. However, along with this fear is the yearning for intimacy. Unfortunately, your prior experiences with relationships have taught you that the only "safe" way to connect is superficially. This gets re-enacted either through the temporary, forced friendship of the blackjack table, or with a sexual partner you don't really know. These behaviors may also communicate a sense of invisibility or "feeling like a loser," a behavior that is both literally and symbolically re-enacted through a gambling addiction.

WRITING EXERCISE: EXPLORING THE DEEPER MEANING OF AN ADDICTION

If you have ever engaged in addictive behaviors as a creative way to cope, take a few minutes to look at the possible ways in which your actions have re-enacted and/or re-storied a prior painful or traumatic experience. Remember to approach this work with non-judgmental curiosity and compassion. Set a timer for 15 minutes. This will prevent you from getting "lost" in the exercise. At the end of 15 minutes if you need more time, re-set the timer for one more 15-minute interval. When you finish be sure to do something that feels soothing such as listening to calming music, drinking a cup of tea, or massaging your hands with scented hand lotion. It is also ok to do something that grounds you in the present, like a household chore, math problems, or wordsearch puzzles.

1) The behavior I engaged in:

_____

_____

_____

What I might have been attempting to re-enact:

_____

_____

_____

What I might have been attempting to re-story:

_____

_____

_____

2) The behavior I engaged in:

_____

_____

_____

What I might have been attempting to re-enact:

_____

_____

_____

What I might have been attempting to re-story:

_____

_____

_____

3) The behavior I engaged in:

_____

_____

_____

What I might have been attempting to re-enact:

_____

_____

_____

What I might have been attempting to re-story:

_____

_____

_____

Acts of Self-Mutilation

As you explore the deeper meaning of self-mutilating behaviors, you may discover that you are using your body to re-enact prior experiences of abuse. Cutting on the upper forearm might represent the place on your body where you were grabbed before you were harmed. If you felt "burned" by parents' abusive words or a lack of protection, you might be replaying that when you burn a part of your body. Picking your lips until they are raw might be interpreted as having to keep secrets and not being allowed to speak. Hurting your hands might make sense to you if your hands were forced to "participate" in sexual molestation.

In addition to injuries providing information about possible physical, sexual, or emotional abuse experiences, you may also be re-enacting perpetrators' threats about what would be done to your body if you ever told anyone about your abuse. Be especially curious about this possibility if you seem to be increasing your self-harm after talking about your trauma in a therapy session or to a trusted person in your life. Think about the possible connections between what *you* do to your body and what your *abuser* threatened to do to you in the past.

Like all other forms of self-destructive behavior, consider the possibility that hurting your body may be a form of self-punishment. Unresolved guilt, shame, and unwarranted self-blame about past trauma and neglect can leave you vulnerable to the idea that you "deserve" to be hurt. When you are lacking in self-compassion, self-harm is always possible.

In terms of re-storying your pain narrative, your acts of self-mutilation might be an attempt to get others to notice your pain. Seeing your cuts, burns, or bruises gives powerful information to friends and family that "something is wrong." This speaks to our natural need for witnesses and the desire to be heard and healed, even when it feels scary to reveal our experiences to others.

Your behaviors may also feel like an opportunity to re-claim a feeling of power and control over your own body. You might relate to the idea that self-mutilation is an opportunity for *you* to decide how, where, and when your body is hurt, rather than that being in the hands of your abuser. It might also be an attempt to get back at the people in your life who have let you down or harmed you in the past. Loved ones do tend to "freak out" when they discover acts of self-harm, and it can be an unconscious way to passive-aggressively "get even" with them for not being there in the past.

When you consider the re-storying aspects of self-mutilation, it's possible that you are trying to hurt your abusers, indirectly, by hurting your own body. This means that as you hurt yourself, you are actually imagining that you are hurting the abuser. This is very common for trauma survivors. One way to check for this is to ask yourself, "whose hand am I cutting or whose body am I hurting?" Be open to the possibility that your deeper intention is to actually hurt the person who hurt you. Since perpetrators are always more powerful than their victims, it makes sense that the normal desire to get back at them and cause them pain could never be realized. Many people believe the "next best thing" is hurting their own body and imagining it's the abuser who is suffering.

You may also be using the injuries as "event markers" to unconsciously validate and remember an unspeakable abuse experience that was forced underground because no one believed you, or it wasn't safe to tell anyone. Oftentimes, scars help us to connect self-harm to a past trauma. They can open the door to remembering where you were, who was with you, and what was happening when you got the impulse to self-harm. Even if you were unable to talk about your experiences, the scar, bruise, or burn reassures and reminds you that the event actually did occur. The injuries serve as a kind of reality check for you, especially when your realities were repeatedly ignored or challenged. The scars also allow others to bear witness to your pain at a future time, when it is safer to feel and reveal it.

When you have ongoing compassion and non-judgmental curiosity about the potentially deeper messages within your behaviors, you will see that they serve a more profound function. This will help you get past your shame. Once you realize you are trying to communicate something important, it opens the door to learning other ways to share your memories and feelings. This allows you to have safe witnesses to your pain without continuing to re-victimize and re-traumatize yourself. Use the following exercise to explore the possible functions of your self-destructive behaviors.

DRAWING AND WRITING EXERCISE: EXPLORING THE DEEPER MEANING OF SELF-MUTILATION

If you have ever engaged in acts of self-mutilation as a creative way to cope, take a few minutes to look at the possible ways in which your actions have re-enacted and/or re-storied a prior painful or traumatic experience. Remember to approach this work with non-judgmental curiosity and compassion. Set a timer for 15 minutes. This will prevent you from getting "lost" in the exercise. At the end of 15 minutes if you need more time, re-set the timer for one more 15-minute interval. When you finish be sure to do something that feels soothing such as listening to calming music, drinking a cup of tea, or massaging your hands with scented hand lotion. It is also ok to do something that grounds you in the present, like a household chore, math problems, or wordsearch puzzles.

1) The behavior I engaged in:

_____

_____

_____

What I might have been attempting to re-enact:

_____

_____

_____

What I might have been attempting to re-story:

_____

_____

_____

2) The behavior I engaged in:

_____

_____

_____

What I might have been attempting to re-enact:

_____

_____

_____

What I might have been attempting to re-story:

_____

_____

_____

3) The behavior I engaged in:

_____

_____

_____

What I might have been attempting to re-enact:

_____

_____

_____

What I might have been attempting to re-story:

_____

_____

_____

If you injure your body, you can also draw the body part that gets harmed and allow yourself to draw the injuries as well. Or you can write about a self-destructive act you engage in. Don't go into too much detail—just identify the behavior.

DRAW THE BODY PART(S) AND INJURIES—FEEL FREE TO ADD WORDS

DRAW THE BODY PART(S) AND INJURIES—FEEL FREE TO ADD WORDS

PART III

WHY "LETTING GO" IS HARD TO DO

The Cycle of Self-Harm

10

LEARNING ABOUT THE "CYCLE" OF SELF-DESTRUCTIVE BEHAVIORS

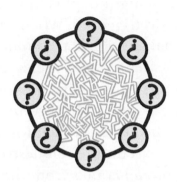

In this chapter we will explore a specific cycle of self-destructive behaviors to help you understand why you feel driven to do the behaviors over and over again. When you are ready, this cycle will also be the roadmap for creative treatment strategies that can be used in place of self-harming acts. As you know, one of the more challenging and scary things about your behavior is that you sometimes feel forced to keep doing it. This can make it more difficult to understand and treat. In truth, these behaviors keep working for you in the *short term*, which is why they can be so hard to stop. Oftentimes a combination of shame, secrecy, and lack of insight can prevent you from making sense out of your actions. In this section of the book you will learn about a "cycle" that will help you identify and understand the inner experiences and dynamics in the environment that trigger the behavior and set you up to go back to it again and again.

When you can visualize and use the cycle in your life it makes it more real, less overwhelming, and can help you achieve a better understanding of self-destructive acts. It also shows that you are not alone in your behavior, which can reduce your anxiety and make it less secretive and shame-based. With a concrete explanation that defines and describes behavior that seems "weird," confusing, and bewildering, you can begin to get back a sense of hope. Processing the cycle allows you to see how the environment, your relationships with other people, and your thoughts and feelings all affect the choice to self-harm. It illustrates how one experience naturally leads to another, and when those experiences are not adequately addressed or short-circuited, self-destructive behaviors become an inevitable response.

An additional benefit to understanding the cycle is that it "makes sense" when you connect it to your family-of-origin. In earlier chapters you learned that when you are exposed to repeated dysfunction and abuse you must create necessary coping skills to survive. Strategies such as hyper-vigilance or staying super-aware of everything around you, dissociating or "spacing out," and self-blame, although life-saving in childhood, leave behind thoughts and feelings that negatively affect you in adulthood. An extreme startle response, "freezing" or "zoning out" when threatened, and an ongoing tape of self-blaming thoughts in your head makes you vulnerable in the world and, therefore, easily triggered. When a trigger, or upsetting reminder of something from your past, takes hold, you cannot stop or change your negative thoughts or feelings, and this leaves you defenseless and sets you up to self-harm.

Once you understand the cycle of self-harm you'll have the opportunity to re-claim control by identifying potential "intervention sites" or places where you can step in and make a new, healthier choice for yourself. Learning to do this will disrupt the cycle and short-circuit the self-destructive behavior. The hopefulness and effectiveness of the model comes from the fact that you are given many opportunities to try something new, even after self-harm has occurred. Although stopping the cycle after the fact will not spare you an injury or the pain of your destructive behavior, it can make it less severe and greatly decreases the likelihood of engaging in that behavior the next time the cycle starts up again.

As we look at the sequence of events that unfolds in the cycle you will have the opportunity to identify how you personally relate to each phase. This will help the model "come to life" and enable you to see how the cycle plays out for you. Keep in mind that the goal is to increase your awareness and understanding of why you do what you do, and to give you new ways to safely achieve those outcomes.

Let's review the different reasons why you might engage in these behaviors. You manage your emotions through distraction, numbing, or a release of endorphins, which are naturally occurring chemicals in your brain that help you feel better. When you do your self-destructive behaviors, you temporarily stop bad thoughts and feelings, punish or re-claim control over the body, or create dissociative or re-grounding responses.

We've also discussed how your actions are a way to re-enact and communicate your pain to others, or to re-story prior abuse and "change the ending." Ultimately, all self-destructive acts are creative attempts to cope with overwhelming thoughts, feelings, and memories. They are cries for help, and ones that deserve to be taken seriously, not ignored. Ironically, behaviors that frighten, confuse, or disgust people may actually be an attempt on your part to engage them. You hope your actions will connect you to significant others, but they often alienate you from them. Clearly, your actions show that you are in pain, and you need something that you're not getting.

When you self-harm you may get the unfair label of being "manipulative," yet these acts represent the only "language" you speak. Taking life-long, invisible, internal pain and making it visible through a cut, burn, drunken state, obese or dramatically under-weight body gives others something to "witness." This means other people "see" your pain, validating experiences that were never "seen" or believed before. In addition to punishing your own body, destructive behaviors are sometimes meant to punish others, leaving them afraid, helpless, angry, and anxious. If you struggle with low self-esteem and no real sense of self, having "symptoms" can be a way to re-claim a sense of "identity."

The challenge for people who love and care about you is to accept that until the behavior is translated, understood, and connected to this cycle, and until you have successfully learned to use new coping strategies and self-soothing techniques, you are unlikely to stop the behaviors. To expect anything else is unreasonable. See if the following example makes sense to you. When you are in pain, you understandably cling to self-harm as if you were clinging to a tiny lifejacket in the middle of the ocean. It's all you have and it's all you know. As far as you are concerned, it keeps you afloat. The desire to have and hold on to a lifejacket is actually appropriate and necessary. It is a basic survival response that is a part of your hardwiring. No one could manage being out in the ocean without one. It doesn't matter to you that this seemingly helpful resource is too small, has lots of holes in it, and may get you into trouble later on. When you are out there struggling, that tiny jacket is the only thing that feels available to you. And you hold on to it for dear life.

Many well-meaning helping professionals demand that you stop your destructive behaviors by forcing you to sign an agreement that you won't hurt yourself. This is typically called a "standard safety contract." Often, they will not let you stay in treatment and threaten to end the therapeutic relationship unless you agree to stop. Some inpatient programs feel strongly about the role contracting plays in treatment, stating that sessions, and even treatment itself, will be terminated if you injure again. This is presented as being in your best interest.

But from your perspective, it's like the helping professional is leaning over the side of a cruise ship and insisting that you turn over the lifejacket you've been using because, "it's not good for you and will make things worse." Understandably, you believe that being in the ocean with no lifejacket at all is far worse. If you've been confronted with this you might resent this insensitive approach, and feel frustrated by the helping professional's position by saying, "What do you know? You're not out in the ocean where I am—you're safe on a cruise ship! You don't understand how much I need this!"

I believe it is actually unfair to ask you to let go of the only "lifejacket" that has kept you afloat. Self-destructive acts can only be reduced and eventually stopped when you are offered other strategies that work just as well. Simply telling you to stop leaves you with no other way to cope. In fact, you know that it usually backfires when other people, frightened or angered by what you are doing, try to pressure you to stop. At best, you might give up your current self-destructive act, and then turn to other forms of self-harm including eating disorders, substance abuse, or unsafe sex.

Therefore, when we look at strategies for treatment in later chapters, you will notice that a "standard safety contract" is not part of the equation. Instead, a model that I call

CARESS—Communicate Alternatively, Release Endorphins, and Self-Soothe—will be offered as a way to work with self-destructive impulses without any power struggles.

However, before we address treatment, this chapter will describe other, safer "lifejackets" that can be swapped with your more complicated and less effective ones. These additional "lifejackets" give you new options for potential "coping strategies" and bring the critical idea of "choice" into the equation. The most important thing to remember is that your *self-destructive behaviors are creative coping strategies, used to calm down your distress, communicate a painful narrative, and provide critical information to helping professionals while offering some short-term self-soothing and relief.*

We've discussed the importance of understanding the meaning behind your self-destructive acts. To do this you must *work with* the behavior rather than engage in power struggles with yourself or others. As stated earlier, looking at your behaviors through a lens of compassion and curiosity becomes the first step in this process. In order for the work to move forward we need a strengths-based perspective rather than a mindset that labels you "sick" or "mentally ill." Rather than focusing on what's "wrong" with you, the focus must be on your courage, strength, and natural ability to heal. You will discover that this mindset is far more effective than a framework that views self-destructive acts as "sick."

You will be reminded to "re-frame" self-destructive acts such as cutting, starving or purging, abusing substances, or engaging in sexually addictive behaviors as inevitable, creative coping strategies that grow out of a history of trauma, pain, neglect, or abuse. Although the behavior is certainly not encouraged, it's understood that repeating the behaviors makes sense, given the fact that your trauma occurred again and again. Or it may be that you keep doing the behaviors because you don't know how else to comfort yourself or communicate your needs.

So, as we move forward, the main focus of our work will be using this cycle, giving you a creative roadmap that will allow you to "short-circuit" the behavior at many different "intervention sites." These interventions can work for you *regardless* of where you are in the cycle of self-harm, which will add a sense of hope to your recovery process.

Although this cycle is experienced by almost everyone who self-harms, the writing exercises will allow you to personalize the model so it uniquely relates to you. Keep in mind that the cycle applies to all forms of self-destructive behavior and can be quite useful in addressing eating disorders, substance abuse and other addictions, gambling, and sexual acting out.

As you learn about the cycle, you will also be able to identify many possible "windows of opportunity" for change. These will offer you new ways to think, feel, and behave. They will move you beyond the "knee-jerk" trauma-based responses you have latched on to in an attempt to feel better. These new options will focus on ego-strengthening, identifying and managing triggers, and working through negative or inaccurate thoughts. They will help you deal with emotions in healthier ways, using strategies to stay "present." You will learn how to increase a sense of internal and external safety, as well as identifying satisfying alternatives to self-injury.

Although I have emphasized the many advantages to doing this work with a well-trained therapist, be sure that your therapist is willing to bear witness to and honor your painful experiences, while using creative treatment techniques that go beyond "talk therapy." They must also be willing to let go of the need to control the pacing of treatment. Most of all, they must believe in the ability of the human spirit to survive and thrive. When you are treated from this mindset, your self-harming behaviors can be truly understood and, in time, become no longer necessary. You can begin to embrace a more positive and accurate sense of yourself when mental health professionals normalize your "symptoms" and struggles, re-framing them as necessary, creative coping strategies.

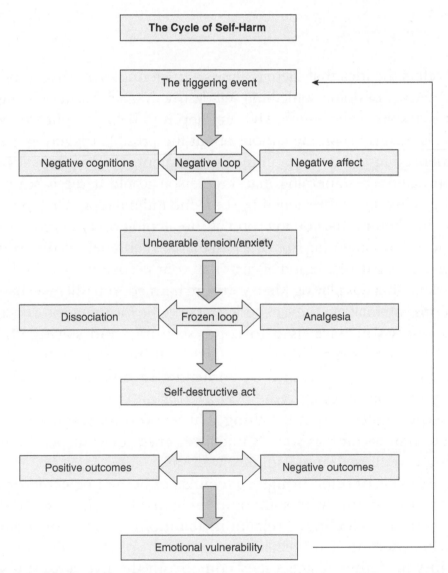

Figure 10.1 **The cycle of self-destructive behaviors.** (*source:* Copyright August 1999 by Lisa R. Ferentz, LCSW-C. Adapted from Alderman, Tracy, *The Scarred Soul: Understanding and Ending Self-Inflicted Violence—A Self-Help Guide,* New Harbinger, Oakland, CA, 1997.)

11

WHAT SETS THE CYCLE IN MOTION?

This model offers the idea that there is always a triggering event that comes before the impulse and the act of doing something self-destructive. Self-harm only happens when you think it is absolutely necessary. The first step is to help you put the behavior into a context. This means becoming curious about the possible triggering events that are either experienced inside of you or in the environment. The trigger may be objectively painful or threatening, something that any person would agree is scary. This could include being yelled at or threatened by someone intimidating. Or the trigger can be a relatively neutral event that you interpret as threatening because your brain and your body associate it with something from the past that was genuinely scary to you. This could include smelling a particular brand of cigar that your perpetrator smoked, or hearing a song on the radio that was playing when you were harmed. You will react based upon the past associations you make to these experiences and the meaning you attach to them.

Given the tools you have used to cope: scanning and staying "hyper-aware" of your environment; becoming easily startled; using your flight/fight or freeze response; along with your inability to handle intense emotional states, it's not surprising that you experience extreme over-arousal and over-reactions to seemingly innocuous experiences. Often the thing that sets you off is not terribly threatening, but what matters most is your "subjective sense" or your personal belief that you are being threatened or are somehow unsafe.

The triggering event often brings up feelings of being neglected or mistreated. When you are interacting with someone, their words, actions, or body language might leave you with a feeling of rejection, abandonment, loss or separation. This is particularly upsetting if it feels like a significant other is disapproving or disappointed in you. Other triggers may come from the five senses: a smell, taste, texture, or something you hear or see. Again, these experiences become threatening because you either consciously or unconsciously associate them with a prior threatening event, an unsafe person, a traumatic or painful experience.

When abuse occurs in childhood, horrible acts are often paired with non-threatening sensory experiences such as a television playing in the background, cooking smells in the kitchen, or leaves falling outside of a bedroom window. Once the brain connects these things with the pain and betrayal of the abuse experience, future exposure to similar sensations will bring back the same emotional responses in you. So, years after your trauma, the same cooking smell in a completely different situation will still bring up feelings of fear or terror. This is further reinforced by the fact that trauma is experienced and stored in the "emotional" part of the brain—the limbic system—which is where our five senses are located. The limbic system is not a reasoning or rational part of our brain so its responses will always be primitive and emotionally based.

Since we are biologically "hard-wired" to respond to something threatening with either flight/fight or freeze reactions, it is understandable that a triggering event sets in motion a "domino effect" of responses in your body that will, in turn, affect your thoughts, feelings, and behaviors. When you become more aware of the concept of "triggering events" you increase your awareness of surroundings, relationships, sensory and body experiences, and thoughts. And you begin to notice how they relate to prior painful experiences and the impulse to self-harm. Once your internal and external triggers are identified, you can create an action plan that helps you avoid, confront, or get way from those triggers.

Part of your forward movement in this work will happen as you begin to personalize the cycle and identify how you specifically experience each phase. With that in mind, after each stage is described, you will have the opportunity to attach your own experiences to the model. If you are working with a mental health professional it will help to process your insights with him or her.

Journaling can be extremely useful because it will make you more aware of what drives your behavior. As you journal and identify the triggers that come before acts of self-harm, you will begin to see patterns and recurring themes. Using the word "REACTS" is a simple way to help you document important information. As you will see, each letter in that word stands for a possible trigger that might influence and set in motion your self-destructive acts.

R: RELATIONSHIP DYNAMICS—Who were you with before you got the impulse to hurt yourself? What were you doing/talking about?

E: EMOTIONS—What were you feeling as you started planning or actually hurting yourself?

A: AWARENESS OF THE FIVE SENSES—What did you smell, hear, see, taste, touch when you had the urge to hurt yourself?

C: CONTEXT—Where were you? What was going on in the environment that might have been upsetting or threatening to you? Include date and time.

T: THOUGHTS—What were you thinking before the act of self-harm?

S: SENSATIONS IN THE BODY—What did you notice happening in your body before you acted on your impulse?

JOURNALING EXERCISE: USING "REACTS" TO IDENTIFY TRIGGERS

Think about a few recent episodes of hurting yourself and see if you can begin to put them into context. This will help you identify the triggers, and make you less vulnerable the next time you are in a potentially threatening situation.

The following is an example to help illustrate the exercise. When you do the exercise, be sure to answer in ways that reflect your experiences. As always, when you finish, be sure to take some time to calm or soothe yourself. You can always refer to Part IV of the workbook for specific suggestions on how to do this if you forget some of the strategies that have already been mentioned.

Example:

My self-destructive act: drinking to the point of getting drunk and being hung over.

R: I was with my 5-year-old daughter. I was trying to get her to go to sleep and she wouldn't stay in her bed.

E: I was feeling overwhelmed and inadequate as a parent, and really angry at my daughter. Then I felt guilty for feeling angry so I wanted to numb myself from those feelings.

A: I heard my daughter crying in her room. I saw myself as a little girl, crying.

C: It was 8:00pm. I was sitting alone in my bedroom. I was triggered by her crying and triggered by feeling helpless and alone in the house.

T: "You know if you drink, the pain will go away." "But if you drink and your daughter needs you in the middle of the night, you might not be able to get up for her." "You see, you really are a bad parent and don't know what you are doing."

S: A lot of tension in my arms, light-headed, stomach is in knots.

1) **My self-destructive act:** _____

R: _____

_____

_____

_____

E: _____

_____

_____

_____

A: _____

_____

_____

_____

C: _____

_____

_____

_____

T: _____

_____

_____

_____

S: _____

_____

_____

_____

2) **My self-destructive act:** _____

R: _____

_____

_____

_____

E: _____

_____

_____

_____

A: _____

_____

_____

_____

C: _____

_____

_____

_____

T: _____

_____

_____

_____

S: _____

_____

_____

_____

12

UNDERSTANDING NEGATIVE THOUGHTS AND FEELINGS

If the triggering event is not addressed, you will move into the next stage of the cycle, which is the onset of negative thoughts and negative feelings. Sometimes, pessimistic thoughts will create negative emotions or your negative feelings will lead to defeating thoughts. You might experience the two together, and when you do it's easy to get overwhelmed by negativity and self-criticism. These thoughts and feelings fuel each other in an endless "negative loop." This part of the cycle is therefore shown with arrows pointing to and from thoughts and feelings.

The thoughts are dangerous and overwhelming in their negativity because they are so distorted. The idea that you become vulnerable to inaccurate and "frozen in time" thinking—placing past experiences onto the present—also makes sense. It is one of the inevitable consequences of childhood trauma. The "learned help-lessness" that may haunt your life keeps you thinking and feeling like a victim. These thoughts and feelings almost take on a life of their own and become your knee-jerk response to triggers.

Trauma survivors are prone to stark contrasts of black and white thinking that plays out as "all or nothing," "always or never." When triggered, your distorted thinking may lead you to say, "This will *always* happen to me," or "It will *never* get better." These thoughts are consistent with childhood concrete thinking, and the powerlessness and hopelessness that comes from being traumatized.

When you are in this part of the cycle, you might also automatically engage in self-blame, exaggerate your missteps, and take ownership of problems that you didn't create. At the same time, you could also downplay your positive contributions and self-worth. Holding yourself unfairly responsible for negative outcomes is a way to reclaim a false sense of control. You may think, "If I caused this problem that means I can come up with a way to fix it."

Instead, this repeats the family-of-origin dynamic of unfairly blaming victims, while the adults take no responsibility for their role in the abuse or neglect. In fact, many abusive adults convince children that *they* are to blame. Children then learn to hold on to and believe those messages of negativity, criticism, and responsibility. Layers of self-hatred and inaccurate self-blame from the past strengthens this phase of the cycle. Unfortunately, thinking you are responsible for events can fuel your negative and distorted sense of self, and sets you up to fail. You cannot fix a problem you did not create in the first place. Adding insult to injury, you can create more guilt if you believe you "should" have been able to fix or change another person or an external event.

Another distorted thought is the irrational belief that if you feel something strongly it must be accurate. In your mind, if you *feel* damaged, responsible, or unworthy, then that becomes evidence that those feelings are true reflections of who you are. When a triggering event brings out a negative thought such as "I am unlovable," you assume the thought must be right. You do not question or re-evaluate its merit. These ideas can create additional negative thoughts and keep you stuck in an endless loop of negativity.

JOURNALING EXERCISE: IDENTIFYING YOUR NEGATIVE THOUGHTS

Take a moment and think about a few recent experiences where you felt the need to do something self-destructive. See if you can record some of the thoughts that might have been present during this part of the cycle. The following is an example to help illustrate the exercise but make sure that you write down the answers that feel right for you. Be sure to calm or soothe yourself afterwards.

Example:

Identify the self-destructive act: <u>cutting my fingers</u>
Identify some of the negative thoughts that surfaced:

- <u>Even though this hurts I feel like I deserve it.</u>
- <u>If people knew I did this they would think I was really weird.</u>
- <u>I hate my hands.</u>

1) Identify the self-destructive act: _____
_____

Identify some of the negative thoughts that surfaced:

_____

_____

_____

2) Identify the self-destructive act: _____
_____

Identify some of the negative thoughts that surfaced:

_____

_____

_____

3) Identify the self-destructive act: _____
_____

Identify some of the negative thoughts that surfaced:

_____

_____

_____

CREATIVE EXERCISE: IDENTIFYING YOUR NEGATIVE THOUGHTS

Another way for you to document your negative thoughts is to make a collage of words you find in magazines. Cut them or tear them out and then glue them to the page below. When you are finished, allow yourself to be curious about the *possibility* that these thoughts are either inaccurate or an exaggeration.

Negative thoughts and the triggering event itself always create negative feelings. Upsetting interactions or self-defeating thoughts would create painful feelings for anyone. But the stakes are much higher if you don't have the basic tools to work through, resolve, and move beyond painful experiences. It is not uncommon for triggers that are reminders of prior abuse or neglect to instantly create anger, depression, despair, or terror. Distorted thoughts can stir up feelings of inadequacy, worthlessness, helplessness, isolation, and powerlessness. Triggering interactions with others can lead to feelings of embarrassment, invalidation, rejection, and betrayal.

One possible reason why you physically hurt yourself may be to get a sense of relief by temporarily reducing emotional upset. Think of the pain as a distraction away from upsetting feelings. As we discussed earlier, if you were not allowed to successfully attach to your primary caretakers you didn't get the internal resources that were needed to manage emotions or undo distorted thoughts. Therefore, doing something self-destructive might be the only way you know how to self-soothe.

Ironically, feeling "negative" or difficult emotions really is doable for anyone! Our capacity to experience a wide range of emotions is part of what makes us human beings. And all feelings, no matter how intense they may seem, always have a beginning, middle, and end. However, the idea that difficulties are time-limited may not be familiar to you if you are a trauma survivor or you have had repeated painful experiences.

You may be afraid to get close to strong feelings because you lack the internal resources that help you navigate or "ride through" the discomfort of powerful emotions. You may not trust your ability to handle emotions without becoming overwhelmed, "falling apart," acting-out, or behaving "inappropriately" so your automatic response to the bubbling up of feelings is to push them away and shut them back down.

WRITING EXERCISE: IDENTIFYING YOUR NEGATIVE FEELINGS

Take a moment and think about a few recent experiences where you felt the need to hurt yourself. See if you can record some of the feelings you might have felt during this part of the cycle. Go slowly, and stop whenever you need to so the work stays manageable. Calm or soothe yourself afterwards. The following is an example to get you started:

Identify the self-destructive act: <u>Bingeing and purging</u>

Identify some of the negative feelings that surfaced:

<u>fear, shame, embarrassment, anxiety. A little bit of feeling powerful and in control, then feeling worried about someone finding out</u>

1) Identify the self-destructive act: _____

_____

Identify some of the negative thoughts that surfaced:

_____

_____

_____

2) Identify the self-destructive act: _____

_____

Identify some of the negative thoughts that surfaced:

_____

_____

_____

3) Identify the self-destructive act: _____

_____

Identify some of the negative thoughts that surfaced:

_____

_____

_____

CREATIVE EXERCISE: IDENTIFYING YOUR NEGATIVE FEELINGS

Use the space below to either draw your feelings—showing them with color, line, and shape—or make a collage of images from magazines that express the emotions that come up for you when you become triggered in this part of the cycle. Calm or soothe yourself afterwards.

13

EXPERIENCING TENSION AND ANXIETY

The growing discomfort that comes from an uncontrollable continual loop of negative thoughts and feelings inevitably brings you to the next stage in the cycle: unbearable tension and anxiety. This stage in the cycle is often experienced as physical sensations in your body, especially when you feel powerless to stop the overwhelming negative thoughts and feelings of despair. You may experience muscle tension, headache, upset stomach, jitteriness, shortness of breath, or heaviness in the chest.

So much of the pain inflicted on victims of physical and sexual abuse lives in the body. As stated earlier, you may mistakenly blame your body for "participating" in sexual acts, particularly if you experienced arousal or orgasm. This can be further fueled by your guilty perpetrator trying to convince you that you "wanted sex" or you "liked it" while it was happening. This can leave you with a deep sense of body betrayal and self-loathing. The rage that cannot safely be expressed towards perpetrators gets held inside and connected to your body instead. Being physically violated can leave you feeling powerless and this loss of control is physically re-experienced when you are overwhelmed with anxiety. Since childhood trauma memories often get "stored" and later felt in the body, it makes sense that you may be more physically vulnerable.

When anxiety goes up, you may feel as if you are "going crazy," which actually increases an already anxious state. Embarrassed, frustrated, and frightened by growing anxiety, you begin to turn inward, yelling at yourself in an attempt to stop the anxious feelings. However, the more you beat yourself up for being anxious the more anxious you become. As anxiety rises there is the additional fear that "it will never end." Consider the possibility that this particular belief is like the commonly held childhood idea that traumatic experience will "never end."

This makes sense, because children have a distorted sense of time and episodes of abuse or pain really do feel like they are going on forever.

Additionally, as you think about and begin to plan for your self-destructive act you may begin to experience "anticipatory anxiety." This is anxiety that comes from a combination of excitement, ambivalence, and guilt since using self-harm to "feel better" is both exhilarating and frightening. If you have a history of hurting yourself you can rely on it to take away bad thoughts and feelings. It is comforting, even thrilling, to experience that immediate relief. You also know there are many disadvantages to self-harm including feelings of guilt, shame, and powerlessness. Perhaps you have promised yourself you will stop or you are fearful of disappointing others. As the internal debate rages the level of anxiety keeps increasing.

WRITING AND DRAWING EXERCISE: IDENTIFYING YOUR EXPERIENCES WITH UNBEARABLE TENSION AND ANXIETY

Think about your recent episodes of self-destructive behavior and the ways in which you experienced anxiety in your body. Make a list of some of the ways you felt anxiety, then see if you can illustrate your anxious state using shapes, line, and color. Calm or soothe yourself afterwards.

Identify the self-destructive acts: _____

_____

_____

Identify some of the sensations you felt in your body as you experienced feelings of tension and anxiety:

1) _____

_____

2) _____

_____

3) _____

_____

4) _____

_____

5) _____

_____

6) _____

_____

7) _____

_____

Now using line, color, and shape as abstractly or concretely as you like, illustrate your state of tension or anxiety:

14

WHAT HAPPENS WHEN YOU "ZONE OUT" AND DON'T FEEL PAIN?

Intense anxiety can actually alter your conscious awareness and leave you feeling genuinely "out of control" and helpless. When you are unable to manage this state the tension becomes unbearable and leads you into the next, inevitable phase of the self-harm cycle, which is the need to zone out or dissociate.

Once you reach this stage of the cycle you are often too overwhelmed to recognize, much less use, healthy external resources. For trauma survivors or people who did not have available resources for comfort, dissociation makes perfect sense because it is a knee-jerk response to extreme threat and stress. It may have been the only reliable way to cope, especially if it helped you to maintain some self-protection in the past. You may have gotten really good at dissociation if you used it throughout your life. When you dissociate a lot, it requires no conscious effort to disconnect from the present moment. Historically, it was a way to mentally escape when you couldn't physically escape. It is designed to reduce tension and provide you with a protective detachment from negative thoughts, feelings, and experiences.

When you zone out you may feel that what's happening around you is surreal, like a dream. This is called de-realization. You can also feel that what's occurring is not happening to your body, almost as if you were standing outside of yourself and watching things happen in a detached way. This is called de-personalization. These states are not unusual for people who often experience dissociation.

When you have a prior history of abuse or neglect and become triggered and overwhelmed in the present, you will quickly go back to a dissociative state. This short-circuits your thoughts and disconnects you from what is happening in your body.

Ironically, the fact that the response has become so automatic for you is what makes it problematic! Before you can think of other ways to respond to threat or stress you are out of your body and "on the ceiling" looking down on the scene. A strategy that once "saved" you in childhood actually disables you in adulthood. You cannot accurately assess a situation or come up with an effective safety strategy if you are frozen like a "deer in the headlights." In this state, you are in a more primitive part of your brain, lacking the ability to reason or problem-solve. You are unable to defend or assert yourself or make healthy behavioral choices.

When you dissociate you are repeating the "freeze" response from childhood. If you were threatened as a child you could not physically fight back or escape. As we discussed earlier, your safest responses were complete stillness, pretending to be asleep, holding your breath, or dissociating to survive the ordeal. No wonder you continue to operate from a "victim mentality" despite the fact that actual abuse is no longer occurring. Powerful coping strategies like dissociation keep you "frozen in time" and unable to distinguish the past from the present.

Dissociation can play a dual role in regards to self-destructive behaviors. Even thinking about the prospect of hurting the body can create a "zoned-out" state. In the short term this may feel like a good option to you. But in the long term, that altered state of consciousness can be scary and take away your power. When those feelings set in, hurting the body can also become a way to *stop* the dissociative state. You may relate to the visual shock and warmth of blood on the skin as a way to re-ground and re-connect you back to an otherwise numb body.

It will help to be able to identify the physical ways in which you experience a dissociative state. It isn't possible to short-circuit them until you understand the sensations in your body that signal the onset of "zoning out."

WRITING AND DRAWING EXERCISE: IDENTIFYING THE WAYS IN WHICH YOU EXPERIENCE DISSOCIATION

Think about your recent episodes of self-destructive behavior and the ways in which you experienced a dissociative state. Make a list of some of the ways you felt "zoned out" or spacey, then see if you can illustrate your dissociative state using shapes, line, and color. Remember to do something that soothes and helps you to feel "present" afterwards. This might include: standing up and moving around, going into a different room, drinking a glass of cold water or splashing some on your face, or taking a warm shower.

Identify the self-destructive acts: _____

_____

_____

Identify some the sensations you felt in your body as you experienced feelings of dissociation or spacing out:

1) _____

_____

2) _____

_____

3) _____

_____

4) _____

_____

5) _____

_____

6) _____

_____

7) _____

_____

Now using line, color, and shape as abstractly or concretely as you like, illustrate your state of dissociation:

You feel a kind of numbness when you're in a dissociative state. You may lose all sense of time, the environment, and your own body. The combination of dissociation and feeling disconnected from your body creates an "analgesic" effect, which means you no longer feel any pain in your body. It's understandable that in a "zoned-out," pain-free state, you can easily hurt yourself in ways you could never do if you were fully feeling your body. Even when you claim you can "feel" the injuring, you are probably not experiencing the pain the way someone else would if they were hurting themselves in a completely present way.

How is it possible to tolerate carving into the skin with a sharp object? Think about the discomfort you feel when you get a paper-cut! Think about what happens if you accidentally touch a hot stovetop. The natural, instinctive response is to immediately pull away from the heat source. It is completely against our biological nature to subject our bodies to painful acts of self-injury. The powerful combination of dissociation (with its accompanying pain-free state), and a prior trauma history (which normalizes hurting the body) make self-harm possible, allowing you to override your protective impulse to pull away from something painful.

JOURNALING EXERCISE: IDENTIFYING YOUR EXPERIENCE WITH ANALGESIA

Think about your recent episodes of self-destructive behavior and the ways in which you experienced analgesia. Remember to do something to soothe and feel "present" afterwards.

1) Identify the self-destructive act: _____

_____

Identify some of the ways you experience analgesia (no pain):

_____

_____

_____

_____

2) Identify the self-destructive act: _____

_____

Identify some of the ways you experience analgesia (no pain):

_____

_____

_____

_____

3) Identify the self-destructive act: _____

_____

Identify some of the ways you experience analgesia (no pain):

_____

_____

_____

_____

15

ENGAGING IN ACTS OF SELF-HARM

Once you are caught in the "frozen loops" of negativity, dissociation, and analgesia, you are primed for the next phase in the cycle: self-harm.

When you zone out you might experience feelings of de-personalization (what's happening is not happening to me) or de-realization (this is not really happening, it's a dream). When you are disconnected from your body the extent to which you injure may not be within your conscious control. Since you don't fully feel pain on your body you are likely to cut deeper or burn more severely than you actually intended when you got the impulse to hurt yourself. You might drink or drug more heavily, binge longer or on more foods, sexually act out further than you wanted to. Ironically, this can leave you feeling *less* in control of your body.

Unfortunately, you might injure yourself in a variety of creative ways. Cutting with sharp objects (knives, scissors, razorblades, pen caps, nail clippers) is the most common method. Most people who self-harm have more than one way of hurting themselves, and you might be able to relate to that. Additional forms of self-harm include: burning; head-banging; limb-hitting and bruising; picking at skin and wounds; trichotillomania (pulling out eyelashes, eyebrows, beard hair, hair on the head, and pubic hair); deep biting; severe scratching; inserting objects into the body; scalding showers; swallowing chemicals; and masturbating to the point of hurting the body. Other behaviors such as limiting calories, bingeing, purging with laxatives, enemas, or self-induced vomiting, unsafe and promiscuous sex, and alcohol and drug abuse should be considered forms of self-harm as well.

As stated earlier, self-destructive behaviors are done in response to profound emotional distress and represent a creative and desperate attempt to re-balance one's emotional state. At this point in the cycle you probably will find yourself over-aroused and incapable of healthy self-soothing and turn to self-harm as a way to re-gain some degree of control over your emotions and your body. One of the primary functions of self-harm is to regulate feelings. It's a coping strategy designed to better control dissociation, over-arousal, and unbearable thoughts that create emotional upset.

As you read in an earlier chapter, in addition to this and other important "functions" served by self-harm, it is always worth exploring the "meaning" and deeper communication of the behavior, keeping in mind that the location and method you use is often not a coincidence and can provide information about your trauma or pain narrative. Remembering that the behavior is a form of communication is essential. Self-harm may feel like the only way you can express your feelings and needs. It's a last resort when you are afraid that direct communication will make you too vulnerable.

This next exercise might be harder for you as it takes a lot of courage to fully identify all the ways in which you engage in self-destructive behaviors. Know that this is an essential step in your recovery journey, and you can go back to this exercise, as needed, to continue exploring your behaviors when you are ready to do so. You can also refer back to the questionnaire you did at the start of the workbook. Remember to do something comforting when you finish this exercise.

JOURNALING EXERCISE: IDENTIFYING YOUR SELF-DESTRUCTIVE BEHAVIORS

Identify your self-destructive acts—try to include how frequently you do them, and when you are most likely to engage in them:

1) self-destructive act:

frequency:

when you are most likely to do the behavior: _____

2) self-destructive act:

frequency:

when you are most likely to do the behavior: _____

_____

_____

_____

3) self-destructive act:

_____

_____

frequency:

_____

_____

_____

when you are most likely to do the behavior: _____

_____

_____

_____

DRAWING EXERCISE: IDENTIFYING YOUR SELF-DESTRUCTIVE BEHAVIORS

Another way you can begin to identify and take ownership of your behaviors is to do a drawing or collage to express them. Use the space below to creatively "name" those behaviors. Use line, shape, and color or cut out words and images that represent your self-harming behaviors and glue them to the page. Calm or soothe yourself afterwards.

16

WHY IT WORKS IN THE SHORT TERM

Once you have engaged in self-harm there are immediate positive outcomes. The behavior is reinforcing because of those short-term "pay-offs" and this is why you return to it again and again. One of the best outcomes is the body's release of *endorphins*, which are naturally occurring opiates or painkillers. When the body has been physically traumatized it is "hard-wired" to respond with these chemicals to help counteract the pain. This endorphin rush reinforces the behavior. You genuinely "feel better" after you hurt yourself and this is exactly what you want to accomplish. Understandably, after the body has been injured the release of opiates produces an intense degree of pleasure that distressed people want to keep re-experiencing.

As you may already know, self-mutilation is not about committing suicide. It's about stopping the pain and feeling better. Once you hurt the body you temporarily feel less depressed, anxious, and tense. It also eliminates the distressing negative thoughts and feelings for a little while. Many people who hurt themselves feel upset before they do it, and then more relaxed, relieved, and calm afterwards.

You may feel re-grounded and re-connected to your body. As mentioned earlier, the shock of seeing blood or the warmth of it on your skin might reassure you that you are alive and help bring you "forward" again. Attention is drawn back to the body when you hurt the nerve-endings in your skin. Part of why reintegration occurs is because wounding the body cuts short a heightened dissociative state. Initially, "leaving the body" feels reassuring and safe. However, dissociating for too long can leave you feeling unsafe, alone, and powerless. As "necessary" as dissociation is, it is equally necessary to have a way to re-connect with yourself, too.

You might have the same experience of re-connecting to your body when you do eating disordered or addictive behaviors. The way to end a dissociative state is to binge or purge to the point of physical pain, nausea, or the release of the food. If you engage in sexual addictions, you might do so to re-connect with your body through sexual arousal and orgasm. If you compulsively gamble and shop you might feel physical sensations of both pleasure and anxiety as you buy another expensive item or place another high stakes bet, but you are grateful and relieved that at least you are feeling something!

You can experience another positive outcome when you use self-destructive behaviors to distract from other unbearable or unresolved issues. You probably devote a significant amount of time to the behavior. Since it is your most reliable coping resource, you might spend time fantasizing and planning for ways to injure your body, buy the food you will binge on, or get the drugs or alcohol you will use to become numb. You might use specific, time-consuming rituals to prepare for the behavior. Time may be devoted to cleansing and caring for the wound after your body has been harmed, just as ritualistic time might be spent before or after a binge or purge. In order to maintain your secret you might also need time to create "cover stories" for injuries, the smell of vomit in the bathroom, or the money missing from the back account.

As time and energy are devoted to thoughts and actions related to self-destructive behaviors, you have less time for other aspects of your life. Self-harming behavior provides an ongoing distraction and helps you avoid uncomfortable memories and feelings. This will make sense to you if you have spent a lifetime downplaying, rationalizing, or denying prior abusive experiences and relationships. When you spend so much time on self-destructive acts, you can't work on dysfunctional relationships, seek out healthier ones, work on self-care, resolve trauma, move forward in your career, or be emotionally available to others. Instead, you are too preoccupied with a secretive, shame-based behavior.

If you were physically or sexually traumatized you understandably felt a loss of control regarding your body. Boundaries were ignored and invaded. You might have experienced physical pain and/or confusing feelings of sexual arousal. Essentially, as a victim your body was at the mercy of the perpetrator. In order to stay safe, you had to comply, perform, and be readily available to meet the needs of your abusers. In your mind, doing self-destructive behaviors might feel like a way to recapture control over your body. In a strange way, choosing to hurt yourself can feel important if you never felt as if your body was your own. As stated earlier, for the first time, you have the power to decide when, where, and how your body will be hurt.

Additionally, you may be re-enacting a learned experience that says, "In order for my body to be comforted, it first has to be hurt." When perpetrators aren't sociopathic, after abusing they may be left with lingering feelings of guilt. Abusers want to get rid of those guilty feelings so they can live with themselves or continue their behaviors. They try to convince themselves that no permanent damage was done and their victims are no longer hurting. In an effort to feel less guilty they try to "comfort" the victim with loving words or non-sexual touch. Perpetrators also want to reduce the likelihood that their victims will tell anyone about the abuse. They attempt to confuse their victims into "liking" what was done to them by "rewarding" them with a treat, present, or extra attention. Although these gifts are confusing, for neglected children who have no consistent resources for healthy attachment, they are necessary and welcome. This repeated experience of being hurt and then being comforted gets imprinted in the brain and body. As a result, the unconscious message that gets normalized is "first you have to tolerate getting hurt before you can get your emotional needs met."

If you relate to this, you might unconsciously re-enact the "pain first—then soothing" experience when you engage in acts of self-mutilation, unsafe sexual practices, and eating disordered behaviors. In order to get the attention, care, comfort, and social engagement you need and crave, you first "abuse" the body and cause it pain.

JOURNALING EXERCISE: IDENTIFYING YOUR POSITIVE OUTCOMES

1) Identify the self-destructive act: _____

_____

Identify some of the ways you experience positive outcomes or pay-offs:

_____

_____

_____

_____

2) Identify the self-destructive act: _____

_____

Identify some of the ways you experience positive outcomes or pay-offs:

_____

_____

_____

_____

3) Identify the self-destructive act: _____

_____

Identify some of the ways you experience positive outcomes or pay-offs:

_____

_____

_____

_____

17

WHY IT DOESN'T WORK IN THE LONG TERM

As you may know, all destructive coping strategies can work in the short term and then eventually lead to negative outcomes. This is an important part of the cycle to process. You might experience a strong sense of powerlessness and helplessness once the initial pay-offs are gone. Ironically, the relief you experience in the short term eventually becomes overshadowed by upsetting outcomes, and you may actually feel worse off in the long run.

You may have little or no memory of actually injuring yourself. This makes sense given the role dissociation plays in the process. You might "awake" to discover your body is injured or bleeding. You might be "standing outside of yourself" while you binge, purge, engage in unwanted sex, or withdraw more money from the ATM to continue gambling. Sadly, if you use self-destructive behaviors to reclaim control you will feel a huge loss of control as you struggle to understand what happened to your body, your finances, or sense of integrity.

This powerlessness is increased when you attempt to stop the behavior only to discover you have done it again. If you experience the symptoms of zoning out during the act you may be unable to stop the cutting, unprotected sex, or eating disordered behavior even if you want to do so. When you are unable to manage your self-harm and do more damage than you intended, you recreate a loss of control over the body and your life, and are left feeling re-victimized.

Another negative outcome is a deepened sense of shame. Like many trauma survivors you may already be vulnerable to this emotion, having bought into your perpetrators' messages of blame. Self-destructive behavior becomes another ugly secret. You feel humiliated and victimized again just like you felt when others hurt you in the past. You probably never talk openly about how you hurt yourself or compromise your safety. You may be afraid of being seen as "weird," "disgusting," out of control, and "damaged." You might not trust others to understand or accept the behavior, partly because you don't really get it or accept it yourself.

Along with shame can be feelings of guilt, disappointment, worthlessness, and self-hatred. Like so many people who engage in these behaviors, you might often attempt to make "pacts" with yourself, loved ones, or your therapist about not acting out again. You are afraid if you reveal another episode of self-harm to others they will be disappointed or angry with you. When you do "relapse" you may struggle with self-loathing, feelings of failure and inadequacy, disappointment, hopelessness, and the genuine concern that you will be rejected or "fired" by your therapist or by loved ones.

When you feel the need to act out, a standard safety contract sets you up for almost certain failure since you signed a contract agreeing to stop and, instead, you've "relapsed." Engaging in your self-destructive behavior again means you've let everyone down, and there may be renewed anxiety about others disapproving of you. Initially you may be convinced the behavior is behind you, and when it reoccurs, it is overwhelmingly disappointing. You might experience feelings of self-hatred, using your "weakness" as proof of your worthlessness.

Since behaviors like self-injury, bingeing, and purging are viewed as anti-social acts, you can feel a deep sense of isolation after engaging in these activities. You are alone in the behavior and alone in its after-effects. You become convinced that no one will be able to understand or help you. The act itself can leave you feeling like you are your own worst enemy. The compulsion to hurt yourself takes you away from family and friends and can create intense conflicts with other people. You might feel forced to stay away from loved ones after acts of self-harm, afraid new wounds or the telltale signs of eating disordered or substance abusing behaviors will be discovered.

Consider that dealing with the issue alone, or having others deny the reality of your pain, becomes a repeat of childhood abuse and neglect. You have to manage something scary, confusing, and shame-based on your own. Self-harm, like childhood trauma, becomes another cross to privately bear.

Just as identifying and owning all of the ways in which you engage in self-destructive behaviors can feel threatening and scary, it is equally hard to agree that there are negative outcomes. When you identify the down side of your actions you are admitting that it may be a problem to keep using them. As we discussed earlier, letting go of these "coping strategies" takes time and a lot of courage. Rest assured that you are still in charge of that decision, even when you admit that there are negative outcomes for you. Remember, this work is supposed to give you greater insight about your actions, not leave you feeling any additional sense of guilt or shame.

JOURNALING EXERICISE: IDENTIFYING YOUR NEGATIVE OUTCOMES

1) Identify the self-destructive act: _____
_____
_____

Identify some of the ways you experience negative outcomes or pay-offs:

_____
_____
_____
_____

2) Identify the self-destructive act: _____
_____
_____

Identify some of the ways you experience negative outcomes or pay-offs:

_____
_____
_____
_____

3) Identify the self-destructive act: _____
_____
_____

Identify some of the ways you experience negative outcomes or pay-offs:

_____
_____
_____
_____

DRAWING EXERCISE: IDENTIFYING THE NEGATIVE OUTCOMES

Use the space below to draw or collage images that represent the negative outcomes you experience or feel when engaging in your self-destructive behaviors. Calm or soothe yourself afterwards.

18

HOW FEELING BAD LEADS TO MORE PAIN

One of the problems with negative outcomes is that they can make you even more vulnerable! The after-effects of self-harm can leave you with new negative thoughts in your head as well as upsetting feelings. These additional experiences can strengthen an existing episode of depression or inaccurate thinking. If guilt and shame were a part of your negative outcomes, those feelings will distort your sense of self and increase your isolation and disconnect from the world. This heightened sense of being alone adds to your emotional vulnerability.

Whatever short-term positive reinforcement you felt when you acted out now disappears and you are left with the more lasting feelings of powerlessness and despair. That negativity is manifested in your body as well. A defeated mindset causes posture to collapse and muscles to tighten or constrict. The non-verbal messages you send get received by others, profoundly shaping and influencing the way other people treat you and what they think of you as well.

In this vulnerable state, the likelihood of being able to successfully and safely connect to others gets reduced. Instead, there is an increased chance of being exploited, ignored, taken advantage of, and not taken seriously. This is a crucial part of the cycle because walking around with cognitive, emotional, and physical vulnerability actually sets you up for the next triggering event.

As you approach people and your environment with a sense of hyper-awareness, suspicion, defensiveness, fear, and anxiety, you are more likely to misinterpret, distort, and personalize innocuous encounters. You will quickly become triggered if you believe situations are threatening when in reality they are not. However, once you get triggered, you are off and running, looping back into the repetitive cycle of self-harm, while others continue to react differently to you as well.

JOURNALING EXERICISE: IDENTIFYING YOUR EMOTIONAL VULNERABILITY

Example:

1) Identify the self-destructive act: <u>burning my forearm</u>

2) Identify some of the ways you experience emotional vulnerability after an act of self-harm: <u>I feel like people notice the burns and I'm afraid they will think I'm weird. I'm less likely to go out with friends or to wear certain clothes that would show my arms. If anyone says anything about it I get really anxious and defensive, and that creates more distance and leaves me feeling more alone.</u>

3) Identify new self-destructive behavior that follows:

   <u>Once I feel more alone, I tend to start drinking to numb the pain, or I go on Craigslist and look for strangers to hook up with, which might lead to unsafe sex.</u>

1) Identify the self-destructive act: _____

   _____

   Identify some of the ways you experience emotional vulnerability after an act of self-harm:

   _____

   _____

   _____

   _____

   Identify new self-destructive behavior that follows: _____

   _____

2) Identify the self-destructive act: _____

_____

Identify some of the ways you experience emotional vulnerability after an act of self-harm:

_____

_____

_____

_____

Identify new self-destructive behavior that follows: _____

_____

3) Identify the self-destructive act: _____

_____

Identify some of the ways you experience emotional vulnerability after an act of self-harm:

_____

_____

_____

_____

Identify new self-destructive behavior that follows: _____

_____

When you can, take some time to review your work. Know that being able to personalize the cycle of self-destructive behavior took tremendous courage. It also indicates a genuine curiosity on your part regarding what you are doing, along with a willingness to move forward by making some meaningful and lasting changes in your life. If you are working with a therapist, share the information you've identified in this chapter. If it feels safe to share it with a trusted and understanding loved one, feel free to do that as well. The most important thing is to review this work with compassion, and to give yourself permission to revisit it and add to it whenever you like.

The next chapter will focus on strategies that allow you to address each part of the cycle, using creative techniques that can help you deal with each stage without feeling that you have to move on to the usual endpoint of hurting yourself.

PART IV

WORKING WITH AND MOVING BEYOND
SELF-DESTRUCTIVE BEHAVIORS

19

WORKING WITH THE CYCLE OF SELF-DESTRUCTIVE BEHAVIORS

The advantage to focusing on a "cycle" of self-destructive behaviors is that it gives you (and your therapist) many potential places to try something different. And any place you intervene can be effective. Since it's important for you to always feel a genuine sense of power and control about the process, you get to choose where you want to first focus your attention in terms of cutting short your destructive behaviors. This model also explores possible treatment options that will ultimately give you a greater sense of control over your body. You will see that addressing any part of the cycle can be useful, and you'll be given many opportunities to practice healthier coping strategies. This sets you up for success rather than the feeling of failure that may be more familiar to you.

In addition, your anxiety about failing gets reduced when you realize there is no wrong place to intervene. This work is often two steps forward and one step back, and you can build on your successes wherever you achieve them. Starting wherever you feel most comfortable allows you to pace the work properly and increases the likelihood that you will make genuine progress. Keep in mind the main ingredients of *compassion* and *curiosity* and you will be able to make whatever changes you choose!

As you learn about the cycle of self-destructive behaviors and all of the possible "intervention sites" notice your ongoing verbal and non-verbal responses (such as a stomachache or muscle tension). This can give you useful feedback about whether or not you still feel overwhelmed or uncertain about introducing a new strategy and if there are areas you are not yet ready to address.

You've already helped to bring the cycle to life by identifying and describing your actual triggering events, negative, distorted thoughts, and upsetting emotions in this workbook. You've been encouraged to identify the specific ways you physically and mentally experience overwhelming anxiety as well as the physical red flags that signal the onset of dissociation. You've shown great strength and courage by naming the different ways in which you engage in self-harm. You understand the importance of identifying and honoring the positive outcomes you experience immediately following your actions, as well as the inevitable negative outcomes that linger afterwards.

You have also identified how this part of the cycle leaves you feeling vulnerable and how that vulnerability affects your thoughts, feelings, and ideas about other people and their intentions. As you work on all of this, you can begin to connect the dots between that vulnerable state and the next triggering event. You have personalized the cycle as a way of honoring your uniqueness, and you've also outlined specific thoughts, feelings, and behaviors that can now be targeted and addressed as you focus on treatment strategies.

As you begin to explore each intervention site and look at some of the creative tools that can be used, keep in mind that most of these techniques can be used interchangeably throughout the cycle. For example, strategies that use visualizations to target negative feelings can also be used effectively to treat distorted thoughts. Art therapy techniques can be applied to many parts of the cycle as well. Breath work is a powerful tool for managing emotions and can also be used to help with triggers and unbearable tension and anxiety. Feel free to experiment with these techniques once you are comfortable with them, applying them to whichever part of the cycle works best.

Although all competent therapists understand the importance of doing treatment, and especially trauma retrieval work, within a trusting therapeutic relationship and a safe clinical environment, it bears repeating. Before moving ahead with any emotionally charged work make sure your therapist helps you put the basics of treatment into place. If you are choosing to not work with a mental health professional at this time pay attention to these same basic principles as it will make the work easier for you to process. These include: your ability to feel stable and grounded; connecting to resources for support; having an image of an internalized "safe place"; and healthy tools for comfort and containment. Let's take a closer look at each of these ingredients.

Feeling stabilized and grounded means that you can better manage emotions when they surface, and you can "stay present" rather than immediately going into a dissociative state when things become uncomfortable for you. Connecting to external resources for support means you have access to things like trustworthy people, concrete services, a spiritual community, a support group, a peaceful and safe environment, or a hobby that gives you a sense of competence. In addition to having access to these resources you also have to feel comfortable reaching out to them and using them when needed.

Developing a "safe place" means using visual imagery to create a picture in your mind that gives you a feeling of peace, comfort, stillness. Once you have that picture, you can "visit it" in your mind's eye, especially when things don't feel particularly safe in the outside world. When you use containment strategies, you are able to "gather up" a difficult emotion and safely put it to the side so it doesn't paralyze or overwhelm you.

You will discover that working with the cycle of self-destructive behaviors will allow you to develop many of these resources and can be the appropriate beginning to more intensive trauma work. Again, I want to remind you that there is no expectation that your destructive behavior will immediately stop. The process takes time, and decisions about reducing or eliminating the behavior must always be in your hands.

20

TREATING THE TRIGGERS

Since the cycle begins with the idea that self-destructive behavior never occurs without a reason, and a triggering event often sets off these behaviors, it makes sense that working with triggers is an important part of treatment. However, you might be so focused on self-destructive acts that you overlook or downplay whatever came before to set things in motion. One way to work on identifying your triggers is to notice when you shift from feeling grounded and present to a state of discomfort or dissociation. This shift can be experienced through thoughts, feelings, or body sensations that get stirred up by situations that remind you of threatening or traumatic experiences from the past. When you reconnect with those experiences you will be triggered and "less present." You may understand the notion of having a flashback but it's helpful to know that flashbacks are not just visual they can also show up through emotions, thoughts, and body sensations.

When you do get triggered, you might chalk it up to being "weird" or "abnormal." You might get labeled "crazy" by friends and family members who see you getting triggered but don't understand why you are upset. They might accuse you of *over-reacting.* Loved ones might become impatient when you can't simply "get over it" and move on. Remember that getting triggered happens automatically and is not proof of any shortcoming on your part. In fact, the goal of treatment isn't "I won't get triggered anymore." I don't think that is a reasonable or a fair goal given the basic survival mechanisms that are hard-wired on everyone's bodies. Instead, *the goal is to recognize when you are being triggered and to learn how to re-ground as quickly as possible,* so you can minimize negative effects such as feeling helpless or "becoming frozen."

In essence, you need to measure your progress by how quickly you *identify and bounce back* from a trigger, not whether or not you got triggered in the first place. Remember triggering does not occur in the "thinking" and reasoning part of the brain (pre-frontal cortex). Rather, it happens in a more primitive part that acts as a smoke alarm or early warning system (limbic system). Therefore, you will not be able to respond with insight when you are triggered. No matter how much your pre-frontal cortex intellectually understands that in your current reality you are safe and not trapped, when triggering experiences set off a fight/flight or freeze response the pre-frontal cortex goes "off-line." This means your reactions are handled by more primitive parts of the brain that are unable to react with higher reasoning skills. Those parts of your brain mistakenly believe you are still unsafe, which is why you might feel powerless and younger when you get triggered.

It is equally important for you to understand the difference between internal and external triggers. Internal triggers come from a *feeling sense* such as nausea, dizziness, butterflies in the stomach, sweaty palms, muscle tightening, or body pain. External triggers often connect to something in the environment that you hear, see, smell, taste, or touch. Oftentimes, an external trigger (smelling your perpetrator's cologne) will set off an internal trigger as well (feeling terrified and helpless inside).

Once you understand the idea of triggering a critical next step is introducing the concept of "context." This means the time of day, date, place, circumstance, and relationship dynamics that are present when you engage in acts of bingeing, purging, cutting, or abusing substances. Initially this is easier to do after the fact, because as you get caught up in planning and carrying out your behaviors you probably won't have an awareness of the internal and external factors that trigger you.

This is a good time to re-visit the REACTS journaling exercise that you did before. It will give you a good idea about the relationship interactions, circumstances, and sensory experiences that trigger you. The following is an example of a REACTS journal entry. It is offered to help you see, in an objective and non-threatening way, the kind of triggers that can operate for people who turn to self-destructive behaviors when they feel overwhelmed. Sometimes, it's easier to first see these dynamics in other people and then you can begin to apply this to your own behaviors.

> Thirty-three-year-old Edith struggled with sexual acting out as well as restricting her calories. She used the REACTS format when she experienced the urge to look for a date with a stranger on Craigslist as well as deny herself any food.
>
> **R:** (RELATIONSHIP DYNAMICS) interacting with my boss at work—he's very demanding—whatever I do, it's not good enough. I was giving him the information he requested, but he didn't validate anything I said.
>
> **E:** (EMOTIONS) invisible, humiliated, inferior, and inadequate
>
> **A:** (AWARENESS OF SENSORY EXPERIENCES) seeing him mock me with his facial expressions, hearing sarcasm in his voice, smelling cigarettes on his breath
>
> **C:** (CONTEXT) alone in his office, after work hours
>
> **T:** (THOUGHTS) "I'm stupid at my job" "No one cares about what I think or say" "I'm not good enough and I'll never be promoted" "He might fire me and I'll lose another job"

"Don't eat dinner—you don't deserve it" "Figure out how to get on his good side" "Go on Craigslist—you'll feel better"

S: (SOMATIC—SENSATIONS ON THE BODY) face is flushed, hands are in fists, leg muscles are tight, knot in stomach, heart is racing, feel sweaty

Once your triggers are identified, you can begin to come up with an action plan to address them. In Edith's case, there were several important internal and external triggers including: the cigarette smell (her perpetrator smoked), being alone with her boss, being made to feel invisible, and struggling with self-doubt and feelings of worthlessness. These were all reminders of past trauma. The anxiety and fear this created in her prompted a knee-jerk response for self-punishment (denying herself food, putting herself at physical risk) as well as a need for comfort and connection (finding someone on Craigslist). You might be able to relate to her struggle in some way.

It's helpful to have several options in regards to triggers. You can explore ways to reduce exposure to toxic triggers, avoid them if possible, or at least think of an "escape clause" so you don't feel like you are being held hostage by people or circumstances that are triggering. The concept of reducing or avoiding triggers may initially feel foreign to you if you are used to simply putting up with experiences that feel awful.

As you think about some of your triggers, you may realize it has never occurred to you that you don't have to be verbally abused by an aggressive boss, or that you're not obligated to spend time with an elderly parent who abused or neglected you in childhood. In addition, you might not realize that it's within your rights to tell a significant other that their perfume or cologne is upsetting you because it's the same scent your perpetrator wore. In these cases, giving you "permission" to limit your time with triggering people, to avoid spending time with them, or, if it's safe, to even confront them about their abusive actions, can all have the effect of giving you back some power and reducing the feelings of helplessness or re-victimization that these experiences create.

Since dramatically changing existing boundaries can feel threatening or overwhelming at first, building on small "baby steps" is the best approach. Start by either reducing the amount of time you spend in potentially triggering situations or by adding an "escape clause." This can include pre-arranging to have a trusted friend or loved one call or text you during the difficult encounter so you have an excuse to step away, re-group, or have a built-in reason to leave if you choose. You can also keep yourself grounded by holding on to your car keys or keeping your keys visible throughout the encounter. Symbolically, car keys are a great reminder of not being trapped or stuck. They also provide you with a visual reminder that says, "You are not little anymore. You are powerful. You can drive—you can leave whenever you want!"

While 45-year-old Stacey had been repeatedly sexually abused in childhood by her father, her mother was a non-protective bystander and denied the abuse ever occurred. As an adult and only child, Stacey was "expected" to continue visiting her parents every Sunday, spending all day in the living room where she had been violated. Since Stacey had learned at a young age that being safe meant being cooperative and she still had a "victim mentality," it never occurred to her that she could say "no" or in any way limit these meetings. After each visit, Stacey would go home in a dissociative state and cut and burn herself. The re-enactment was feeling "cut down to size" by her father's abuse and "burned" by her mother's denial. The triggers related to all of the sights, sounds, and smells of her childhood home. Addressing this part of the cycle meant working to reduce the triggers by limiting the amount of time she spent with parents, pre-arranging to have cell phone "interruptions" so she could get a break from the triggers, and insisting that the family gatherings happen in a "neutral" restaurant. Eventually, Stacey was able to skip some of the Sunday meetings. This was a huge accomplishment for her and helped her re-claim a sense of power and control. The ending is even more hopeful. After finding the courage to confront her father about the abuse and again being met with denial, Stacey made the decision to end her family visits. When she did, her self-destructive behaviors completely stopped!

If possible, when you must attend a gathering or function "scope out" the space ahead of time. Sit facing the doorway and/or find a seat closest to the exit, and make sure that no one is seated behind you. All of these small things can increase your sense of safety and reduce the likelihood of getting triggered.

In time, you can experiment with more direct limit setting. This can include shortening the length of an uncomfortable encounter or even refusing to participate in conversations or events that feel unsafe. As you work to reduce the triggers in your life and begin to feel less hijacked by them, the cycle of self-destructive behaviors can potentially be short-circuited in its earliest stages. When you avoid triggers or rebound from them more quickly, you stay grounded and present, and spare yourself the negative thoughts and feelings that can take away your power.

WRITING EXERCISE: COMING UP WITH NEW BOUNDARIES OR AN ESCAPE PLAN

Take a moment and think about a situation that might be triggering for you. See if you can come up with a plan to limit, reduce, or avoid that encounter. If it helps, ask a trusted friend or therapist to suggest additional ways to set limits. Notice how it feels when you give yourself permission to change the boundaries.

A1) Identify a situation or personal encounter that could be triggering:

_____

_____

_____

_____

_____

2) Identify the things that might trigger you:

_____

_____

_____

_____

3) Describe a potential "escape plan"—ways to reduce the triggering or a new strategy to avoid the triggering event or interaction:

_____

_____

_____

_____

4) Identify the thoughts, feelings, and body sensations that you experience when you give yourself permission to create this new plan:

_____

_____

_____

_____

_____

B1) Identify a situation or personal encounter that could be triggering:

_____

_____

_____

_____

_____

2) Identify the things that might trigger you:

_____

_____

_____

_____

_____

3) Describe a potential "escape plan"—ways to reduce the triggering or a new strategy to avoid the triggering event or interaction:

_____

_____

_____

_____

_____

4) Identify the thoughts, feelings, and body sensations that you experience when you give yourself permission to create this new plan:

_____

_____

_____

_____

_____

21

DEALING WITH NEGATIVE THOUGHTS

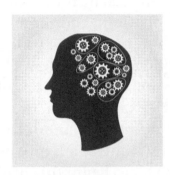

Given the way the cycle of self-destructive behaviors works, when you are unable to re-ground from triggering you will likely begin to experience thoughts that are negative and distorted. Ironically, the fact that your thoughts are not rooted in present reality doesn't matter. They are experienced as real because they hijack your thoughts and reflect distorted beliefs that challenge your self-worth and connect with earlier traumatic experiences. Therefore, these thoughts *must be identified and challenged as either inaccurate, distorted, an assumption, an exaggeration, a necessary coping strategy, or someone else's beliefs.* Once these new possibilities are considered you can re-frame the thought and come up with a more accurate and less destructive replacement. This becomes another "intervention site" within the cycle of self-destructive behaviors.

Look for the typical thought distortions that were identified in an early chapter including: downplaying your accomplishments and exaggerating your mistakes; believing that an emotion is true because you feel it; black/white, all/nothing thoughts; making assumptions about what other people think; and over-generalizing (believing if something happened once, it will keep happening).

As you work with this part of the cycle it helps to begin identifying the most common inaccurate or judgmental thoughts that go with your acts of self-harm. Most people have a tape that plays in their mind like an endless loop, with the same set of negative messages dominating their thoughts. When you really look at it, you'll realize that these messages have been operating in your head for a very long time. Once you've identified your most common negative thoughts, it helps to label them as exaggerations, assumptions, or distortions. This is an important step in re-teaching your brain to challenge what you have been automatically accepting as "truth." Keep in mind that these messages were probably given to you by adults you loved and trusted, which is why you never questioned them in the first place.

A common example of a negative and distorted thought for someone who engages in self-destructive behavior is "I am bad." Being open to the very real possibility that this is a distorted, exaggerated thought, or a necessary coping strategy that allowed you to stay loyal to an abuser, allows you to step back. This creates a new opportunity to re-evaluate the accuracy of your thinking. This is a critical part of treatment as feelings and behavioral choices are often the byproducts of your thoughts. When you can learn to re-examine your mindset you are often spared the destructive, negative experiences that follow.

Once you have identified your negative thought and labeled it a distortion, someone else's perspective, an exaggeration, or a false belief, you can begin to explore a healthier re-frame or a replacement for the original thought. "I am bad" can be re-framed as "Something bad happened to me, I am not bad." The writing exercise below allows you to begin this process of identifying, challenging, and then re-framing the thoughts that often kick in when you get triggered. You can refer back to your earlier journal entries that related to self-blaming thoughts, or the negative thoughts you documented when you became aware of the impulse to hurt yourself. There may be additional thoughts that you can access when you think about this idea of a negative childhood tape.

After writing the automatic thought, write a new thought, or re-frame, in larger print or even a different color, to make it stand out and override the old thought. Whenever you become consciously aware of your negative thoughts you can quickly read the re-frames and retrain your brain to go to a more accurate, positive thought. This, in turn, can go a long way towards ending the self-destructive cycle by preventing your negative thoughts from leading to overwhelming feelings and unmanageable anxiety.

Carl had a long-standing history of abusing pot and repeatedly cheating on his girlfriends as well as several past wives. After a lifetime of blaming his behavior on others, he learned, through the course of group therapy, to take responsibility for his actions. However, in doing so, he was left with thoughts that humiliated and shamed him. Not surprisingly, as a result, his substance abuse increased. Working on his distorted thoughts became a major focus of treatment since they triggered the emotional pain that fueled his "need" to get high. He identified his five most common negative thoughts and then practiced countering them with more accurate re-frames.

After all the hurt I've caused, I don't deserve to be sober

I have taken responsibility for the hurt and made amends. I have the right to be healthy and sober

If I get high it won't make any difference

Getting high deeply affects every aspect of my life

Cheating in all of my relationships means I am worthless

Cheating in all of my relationships was a sign of my unresolved issues with attachment and loss. I am a worthwhile human being

I will always feel depressed and my life will never get better

There are times when I am not depressed, and that shows me my life is actually improving

Getting stoned will take away my pain

Getting stoned brings more pain into my life and leaves me feeling out of control

Take a moment to notice how Carl's new thoughts are able to challenge his exaggerations and inaccurate thinking, and how his re-frames are so much more hopeful and affirming than the messages from the old "tape."

WRITING EXERCISE: COMING UP WITH NEW RE-FRAMES FOR NEGATIVE THOUGHTS

A1) Identify a common negative thought that plays on your "tape" when you get triggered:

_____

_____

_____

2) Challenge the thought by writing about why it could be inaccurate, distorted, an assumption, an exaggeration, or someone else's perspective:

_____

_____

_____

_____

_____

_____

3) Write a new, more accurate thought to replace the old one (use bigger letters and a different color):

_____

_____

_____

_____

_____

4) Identify the thoughts, feelings, and body sensations that you experience when you give yourself permission to think this new thought:

_____

_____

_____

_____

_____

_____

B1) Identify a common negative thought that plays on your "tape" when you get triggered:

_____

_____

_____

2) Challenge the thought by writing about why it could be inaccurate, distorted, an assumption, an exaggeration, or someone else's perspective:

_____

_____

_____

_____

_____

_____

3) Write a new, more accurate thought to replace the old one (use bigger letters and a different color):

_____

_____

_____

_____

_____

_____

4) Identify the thoughts, feelings, and body sensations that you experience when you give yourself permission to think this new thought:

_____

_____

_____

_____

_____

_____

C1) Identify a common negative thought that plays on your "tape" when you get triggered:

_____

_____

_____

2) Challenge the thought by writing about why it could be inaccurate, distorted, an assumption, an exaggeration, or someone else's perspective:

_____

_____

_____

_____

_____

3) Write a new, more accurate thought to replace the old one (use bigger letters and a different color):

_____

_____

_____

_____

_____

4) Identify the thoughts, feelings, and body sensations that you experience when you give yourself permission to think this new thought:

_____

_____

_____

_____

_____

Once you have new "re-frames" to challenge and correct the old thoughts, strengthen your progress even more by putting those re-frames on a brightly colored index card or large Post-it. This lets you carry them in your pocketbook or wallet, attach them to a bathroom mirror, dashboard, inside of a desk drawer at work, or on the refrigerator. Seeing the brightly colored card becomes an additional reminder for you and continues to retrain your brain to exchange negative thoughts with new ones that create a sense of hope.

Another intervention to try at this point in the cycle is a thought-stopping strategy that can help you with your upsetting or overwhelming thoughts. Unfortunately, classic thought-stopping techniques, like snapping a rubber band on your wrist, although effective, are meant to distract you by inflicting physical pain. Obviously these strategies are not recommended because you already hurt yourself! Additionally, saying "No!" or "Stop thinking that thought!' can create an internal battle that makes you feel worse.

Instead, I have created a simple thought-stopping technique that you will find effective because it spares you the internal debate, and feels more doable than bullying yourself into stopping distressing thoughts. When an overwhelming and uncomfortable thought kicks in, rather than tensing up and fighting it, simply say "Not now." At the same time extend your arms in front of you, palms facing in to each other, and then move your arms all the way to the left of your body and out of your direct line of vision. This is a non-verbal message to the brain that the thought is being "put to the side" rather than allowing it to stay front and center in the mind. The left side of your body is also representative of the past and is another way to symbolize not holding onto the thought in the present moment. "Not now" as opposed to "No!" or "stop thinking that" is a gentler way for you to temporarily dismiss your unwanted thoughts. The more you practice this strategy, the easier and more effective it will become.

> Behavioral Exercise: Choose an uncomfortable thought, practice saying "not now" while moving your arms to the left

Another strategy that you can use in this part of the cycle is a simple visualization I've created called "the paint roller technique." Imagine a large paint roller and a pan of brightly colored paint. Choose a color that you find soothing. Since this is special paint, imagine that it has a wonderful fragrance to it as well. As the thoughts continue to present themselves, imagine that the paint roller is dipped in the pan and then gently rolls across and over them. With your eyes, follow the movement of the roller: either back and forth, from left to right, or up and down. It helps to match the rhythm of breathing in and breathing out with the movement of the paint roller. Slowly inhale, watching the roller move in one direction then slowly exhale as it moves to the opposite direction. You can use as many "coats of paint" as needed until the thought is completely covered over by the soothing paint color. Allow yourself to notice the pleasing fragrance and let that soothe you, too. You will be avoiding an internal power struggle by allowing the thoughts to "just be there" as they are painted over by the roller.

> Behavioral Exercise: Choose an uncomfortable thought and then practice the paint roller technique

If you respond well to simple thought-stopping techniques and don't feel triggered by the word "stop" you can visualize, draw, or look at a picture of a stop sign, or actually carry a child's toy stop sign in your pocket. This also reminds the brain to "step on the brakes" when a negative thought surfaces.

There are other equally effective strategies that allow you to re-evaluate a destructive thought. If you like the idea of analyzing your thoughts, you can do a simple writing exercise that will help you identify what you gain by holding on to a negative thought compared to the emotional or behavioral price you pay for continuing to believe that thought. The price you pay for buying into thoughts that put you down can be very steep. Negative thinking can take away hope, and increase low self-worth and shame as well as other draining symptoms of depression. It puts a limitation on your personal growth and sets you up to be re-victimized.

Processing the ways in which you *gain something* from negative, distorted, or judgmental thoughts may seem less obvious, but like most people, you probably don't hold on to thoughts unless you get something from them. In many cases, the inner voice that puts us down thinks it's somehow being protective. Despite the fact that your inner thoughts are critical, shaming, controlling, demanding, or perfectionistic, they might "protect" you by trying to keep you from failing, disappointing others, or taking risks that would potentially lead to loss, rejection, or ridicule. Ironically, it might feel safer to put yourself down and tell yourself that you can't do something, than to try something new, and not have it work out or have someone else chastise you. It's worth taking the time to consider both the advantages and disadvantages to negative thinking as this can help you make a better decision about whether or not those thoughts should be held onto or finally let go. The following exercise is adapted from the well-known cognitive therapist, David Burns.

Twenty-seven-year-old Daniel has had a serious gambling addiction. Not surprisingly, it has led to the break-up of several meaningful relationships in his life. Digging deeper, he finds the distorted belief, "I am unworthy of love" and realizes his addiction is a way to sabotage the relationships he doesn't think he deserves to have. He then uses the strategy of processing the advantages and disadvantages to holding on to the core belief that keeps his addiction going.

I am unworthy of love

DISADVANTAGE TO THINKING IT

I feel shame

It keeps me alone in the world

I feel different from other people

I sabotage my relationships

Sets me up to hurt myself

It deprives me of a support system

It leaves me feeling depressed and hopeless

Forces me to get the rush from gambling

ADVANTAGE TO THINKING IT

It protects me from rejection

Keeps distance = I won't get hurt

I don't have to be social

Not marrying = won't get divorced

WRITING EXERCISE: IDENTIFYING THE ADVANTAGES AND DISADVANTAGES TO YOUR NEGATIVE THOUGHTS

1) Write out a common negative thought:

_____

_____

_____

THE ADVANTAGES: **THE DISADVANTAGES:**

2) Write out a common negative thought:

_____

_____

_____

THE ADVANTAGES: **THE DISADVANTAGES:**

3) Write out a common negative thought:

_____

_____

_____

THE ADVANTAGES: **THE DISADVANTAGES:**

Another strategy to try at this part of the cycle is to consider the difference between the way you think about and talk to yourself, versus the way you talk to others. The difference can be striking. You are probably quite forgiving, accepting, patient, and non-judgmental of others in ways you never apply to yourself! The value of focusing on this is not to create shame or guilt, but rather to show that you are quite capable of thinking thoughts that are kind, supportive, and loving. If you struggle with the idea that you deserve the same non-judgmental treatment you show others, consider that your hurt "inner child" needs and deserves to be treated with kindness.

When you have been repeatedly abused or neglected in childhood, you hold onto messages from your perpetrator that produce feelings of blame, shame, or disgust. This makes up the "tape" that plays in your head throughout your lifetime. I believe that there is nothing more powerful than the way we talk to ourselves about ourselves. We have a non-stop tape that reminds us of who we are and how we do or don't deserve to be treated in the world.

Making a new "tape" is a critical intervention. On this tape the messages must be loving, kind, and uplifting, supporting self-worth, and enhancing self-esteem. Engaging in any kind of self-destructive behavior will not fit with this new tape. You might need help in "scripting" a more positive tape if you don't speak the language of self-love and self-care. If you are unable to put enough loving and supportive thoughts on your tape, think about a person or pet from your past or present who unconditionally cares about you. That person or pet might be readily available in your mind: a deceased grandparent, your third grade math teacher, a friend's parent from childhood, a beloved cat or dog.

If you cannot identify anyone who cared about you (although there typically is someone, because you probably wouldn't still be alive or nearly as high functioning if NO ONE cared about you) think of a loving character from T.V., a book, or a movie. You can probably imagine positive messages that would come from that character. Use those words for your tape.

WRITING EXERCISE: MAKING A NEW POSITIVE TAPE

Take a few minutes and get comfortable, then think about the positive messages you'd like to put on a new tape that plays in your mind. You can bring in your own loving thoughts or add messages that would come from people in your life who believe in you and would be able to contribute in positive ways to your tape. Now allow yourself to "script" those new messages. If this still feels hard for you to do, think about creating a script that you would give to a child or someone you admire.

_____

_____

_____

_____

_____

_____

_____

_____

_____

_____

_____

_____

_____

_____

_____

_____

_____

_____

_____

You can bring this to an even deeper level by making an actual tape recording of the loving messages. Again, if you are working with a therapist you may ask him or her to make the tape for you, particularly if you find their voice soothing, comforting, and believable. This is a good first step. The eventual goal is for you to make the recording with your own voice. This makes the experience more authentic and addresses the idea that there is nothing more important and powerful than the way you talk to yourself about yourself. Messages such as "I deserve to be happy," "I deserve support for my pain," "There are things in my life that I can control," or "I can focus on gratitude" are all new thoughts that can be put on your healing tape.

> Behavioral Exercise: Make a tape recording from the script you have written above

22

MANAGING NEGATIVE FEELINGS

If you are unwilling or uninterested in addressing the parts of the cycle that focus on triggers or negative thoughts, you can focus on learning how to manage your emotions. This is a critical place to intervene because given your potential issues with attachment and its long-term affect on regulating moods you may often be vulnerable to feeling easily overwhelmed by your emotions. Through no fault of your own, the fact that you may be lacking the necessary internal resources to self-soothe or re-ground adds to your distress. Keep in mind that one of the major reasons why people hurt themselves is to try to manage frightening or overwhelming feelings.

When you work on this part of the cycle you will begin to feel a sense of confidence and reassurance about your ability to manage difficult emotions such as despair, rage, hopelessness, and helplessness. Once you feel more capable of handling these feelings you become less anxious and less afraid of them. This dramatically reduces the need to keep pushing feelings back down or to short-circuit them with distracting or numbing behaviors.

Think about a small child who is running and falls and is suddenly overcome with physical pain and emotional distress. If that child has a secure attachment to a loving, available caretaker they will experience a parent quickly coming to their aid. In addition to physical comfort and soothing words of reassurance parents also label the experience for the child, attaching feeling words that help the child gain an understanding of what they are emotionally experiencing.

In this scenario, Mom or Dad might say, "It's ok, Timmy, I know you feel sad, because you fell down and that really hurts! I'm here now and everything will be okay. Let's go put a band aid on it and we'll make it feel better." As this unfolds, Timmy can take in his parent's description of what has happened. He is feeling hurt and sad and a trusting caretaker is validating his right to have these emotions. The parent is also offering him the reassurance that he will feel better soon.

What would happen if instead Timmy's parent ignored his pain saying, "That doesn't hurt!" or yelled at him to "Stop acting like a baby and get up off the ground"? Aside from the obvious lack of comfort and shaming this would produce, it also deprives Timmy of an opportunity to label and understand his feelings. In many cases, abusive parents downplay or cancel out emotions by saying to their victims "Nothing hurtful is happening," which leaves children with confusing messages about whether or not their feelings are justified or accurate.

As you address this part of the cycle, it is important to first acknowledge and validate your emotional states before moving in the direction of shifting them. In a prior chapter, you identified some of the emotions you feel when you get triggered and consider turning to a self-destructive act. Take a moment and re-visit that journal entry and allow your own voice to validate the feelings that may not have been noticed or supported throughout your childhood. If you grew up with parents who did not take the time to comfort or explain emotions you will begin to realize how important it is to learn or re-claim an "emotional vocabulary."

> Forty-five-year-old Amanda's childhood story strongly illustrates this issue. She grew up in a family with an emotionally shut down father and a mother with a serious addiction to prescription drugs. She has many memories of her mother "passed out on the living room floor, half undressed, while her father sat on the sofa reading the newspaper as if nothing was wrong." After repeated failed attempts to get a response from her father, Amanda stopped trusting her feelings of terror and despair and started to discount them, like her father did. She learned to survive what was happening by "permanently shutting down her feelings and becoming numb like her Dad." She accomplished this by developing a drinking problem and bulimia. As she continued to grow up, somewhere in the back of her mind she realized that "she no longer had words for her feelings and felt numb most of the time."

Many survivors of early trauma, neglect, or abuse are unable to put words to their emotions because caretakers did not label their experiences for them. You may still struggle with this when a therapist, significant other, friend, or colleague asks how you feel about something and all you can do is respond with a shrug of your shoulders. The people in your life might misinterpret your lack of response as disinterest or disrespect, when in fact you really can't put into words what you are feeling or needing in that moment. This is not only frustrating for those who interact with you, it can be deeply frustrating for you, increasing a sense of inadequacy, anxiety, or shame.

However, there is good news: you are fully capable of learning an emotional vocabulary at any stage of life. Once you have a better grasp of some of the words that can be used to describe emotional states, you can begin to apply them to different situations and interactions. Take a moment and read some of the feeling words listed below, then choose the ones you relate to and see if you can begin to identify situations where those emotions might come into play for you. Feel free to add other feeling words to your list.

WRITTEN EXERCISE: CONNECTING FEELINGS TO A VARIETY OF SITUATIONS

Upset	Worried	Anxious	Unsure	Tense
Angry	Peaceful	Joyful	Accepting	Numb
Comfortable	Protected	Generous	Alive	Weird
Embarrassed	Happy	Concerned	Pleased	Kind
Proud	Jealous	Brave	Blue	Mad
Unloved	Hateful	Elated	Cautious	Calm
Afraid	Amazed	Patient	Free	Shaky
Impulsive	Overwhelmed	Compassionate	Loving	Sad
Curious	Sarcastic	Coddled	Animated	Shy
Surprised	Nurtured	Funny	Lucky	Ugly
Inadequate	Sorrowful	Nervous	Playful	Cold
Beautiful	Distressed	Misunderstood	Responsible	Crazy
Content	Respected	Confused	Moody	Bold
Entertained	Moved	Grounded	Relaxed	Dull
Insecure	Agitated	Passionate	Strong	Guilty
Ignored	Honored	Condescending	Bubbly	Jumpy
Nurturing	Supported	Hated	Lost	Lazy
Sexy	Attractive	Threatened	Lonely	Safe
Capable	Offended	Qualified	Discouraged	Phony
Protective	Flirty	Validated	Excited	Daring
Triggered	Hurt	Attacked	Weak	Jaded
Humbled	Cheerful	Grateful	Timid	Quiet
Speechless	Superior	Suspicious	Giddy	Pushy
Inferior	Bothered	Spiritual	Sorry	Sick
Badgered	Intimate	Tired	Shaken	Witty
Admired	Competitive	Impatient	Alarmed	Young
Exhausted	Enraged	Satisfied	Hopeful	Tough
Invisible	Mocked	Hysterical	Furious	Old
Patient	Romantic	Childish	Horrified	Silly
Mature	Smart	Foolish	Bored	Naive

1) identify a feeling: _____

   connect to a situation or interaction:

   _____

   _____

   _____

2) identify a feeling: _____

   connect to a situation or interaction:

   _____

   _____

   _____

3) identify a feeling: _____

   connect to a situation or interaction:

   _____

   _____

   _____

4) identify a feeling: _____

   connect to a situation or interaction:

   _____

   _____

   _____

You can also keep a daily log of simple feeling words as you become aware of the different emotions you experience throughout the day and the week. This reinforces that you actually have a wide range of feelings—probably more than you realized. Documenting them will increase your awareness of different moods, while also validating everything you feel. Keep in mind there are no "bad" feelings. All feelings are okay! What's important is what you do with them and how you express them.

WRITTEN EXERCISE: DAILY LOG OF FEELINGS

SUNDAY:

_____   _____

_____   _____

_____   _____

_____   _____

_____   _____

_____   _____

MONDAY:

_____   _____

_____   _____

_____   _____

_____   _____

_____   _____

TUESDAY:

_____   _____

_____   _____

_____   _____

_____   _____

_____   _____

WEDNESDAY:

_____

_____

_____

_____

_____

THURSDAY:

_____

_____

_____

_____

_____

FRIDAY:

_____

_____

_____

_____

_____

SATURDAY:

_____

_____

_____

_____

_____

In addition to written exercises that help identify and honor your different emotional states, you can also document and explore feelings through artwork. If "performance anxiety" gets in the way because you don't like the way you draw, focus on simpler, abstract representations using colors, shapes, and lines to express your varying emotions. You can even just use scribbling to release and show feelings.

If you grew up in an environment that didn't allow for the open, safe expression of feelings, or you are currently in a relationship that doesn't encourage emotional sharing and processing, it is even more important to have your own personal emotional outlets.

Many trauma survivors walk around with unprocessed shame, guilt, and blame. These are important emotions that negatively impact thoughts, behaviors, and self-esteem when they are not addressed. The more you are able to identify, appropriately express, and resolve your emotions, the less you will need to numb them through self-destructive acts. Safely processing these emotions, both verbally and through art, is critically important to your healing and gives you another way to "show" others your pain narratives.

If you are concerned about the possibility of becoming dissociated or triggered during any of these exercises it will help to set a timer for 10 minutes. This external re-grounding resource (the sound of the timer going off) will ensure that you don't get "lost" in the project. If after 10 minutes you are still feeling comfortable, re-set the timer and continue the work for another specific block of time. Always give yourself permission to stop. You do not need to complete any of these assignments in one sitting. Calm and soothe yourself afterwards.

DRAWING EXERCISE: USING LINE, SHAPE, AND COLOR TO EXPRESS EMOTIONS

Using crayons, colored pencils, or magic markers, draw simple representations of the following common emotions—using line, shape, and colors.

ANXIOUS

HAPPY

ANGRY

SAD

AFRAID

CALM

CONFUSED

PROUD

LOVING

EMPOWERED

TIRED

COMFORTED

SAFE

You can also use the technique of collaging by choosing words and images from magazines that represent your different emotional states. If there is the possibility of cutting yourself, try tearing the images out of magazines rather than using a scissor. Once you have found the words and pictures that capture what you are feeling, take some time to arrange them on the page and then use a glue stick to hold them in place. You might want to refer back to the emotions you identified in the early part of the self-destructive cycle.

COLLAGE EXERCISE: USING IMAGES AND WORDS FROM MAGAZINES TO EXPRESS EMOTIONS

THE EMOTION: _____

THE EMOTION: _____

THE EMOTION: _____

Once you are able to identify feelings, you can begin to learn the skills of "affect regulation" or safely managing emotions. Remember it's not your fault that you may be lacking healthy strategies, and you deserve support and guidance in learning how to navigate feelings. As you begin to work with your emotions keep in mind that the expression of feeling can bring up a lot of thoughts and memories. In your family of origin it's possible that the display of emotion was represented by two opposite extremes: a parent who was "out of control" with their feelings and a "shut down" parent who expressed nothing. If this was your situation you will have legitimate concerns about not wanting to look like or act like the parent who could not regulate or control their emotions.

Sixteen-year-old Lacey illustrates this dilemma when she says, "My Dad goes out gambling and when he comes back, if he's lost a lot of money he starts screaming at us. He can stay in a really bad mood, yelling at us for days, until he goes out and wins some of the money back. My Mom doesn't fight back or yell at him. She just takes it and tells us not to do anything to upset him even more. If my younger brother asks her to make my father stop, it's like she doesn't hear him. She's just blank. Sometimes my brother starts to act like my father and he becomes a screaming crazy person. But I never want to turn into my father, so when I start to feel angry and stuff I try to be blank like my Mom. When the feelings are too strong I cut myself. That helps me to go blank.

As you move forward with this work remember that there is a difference between feelings and actions. You can get in touch with emotions and still choose to not act on them in any way. However, if you have buried your feelings for a long time it is important to learn how to safely and appropriately express yourself. You may need ongoing reassurance that as you reconnect with feelings the "dam won't break," and you won't be left feeling flooded and overwhelmed.

One way to get that reassurance is to learn how to balance the expression of feelings with the ability to also contain them when necessary. There is a difference between containing feelings and *repressing* them. If you are good at "putting away feelings" it may be because trusted family members modeled this by zoning out and shutting down in order to stay safe. Once you find the courage to re-connect with and express feelings, you don't want them shoved back in the bottom drawer where they will be denied or forgotten again.

By the same token, it's important to know that you will not be hijacked by your feelings. If you fear that the floodgates will break, you may worry about drowning in a never-ending river of emotion. This is where strategies for containment are really helpful. This means *creating a safe way to set aside the things that might feel overwhelming until you are ready to re-visit them.* When you have this skill the emotional work can stay manageable. Think in terms of a two-step process when working with this part of the cycle. It is important to safely express feelings, and then just as important to sufficiently contain them so flooding doesn't occur.

One strategy I have created to assist with your emotions is targeting a feeling you want to contain, gathering it up, and then representing it by visualizing it as a shape and a color. Then take that image and think about a bigger container you can put it into, adding as many additional layers of containment as you need, until the original feeling is fully stored away and no longer taking over your thoughts or behaviors. By creating your own images you are reinforcing the idea that healing resources can be found within yourself. The following example will make this strategy clearer for you.

> Fifty-two-year-old Maria has been struggling with anger for most of her life. Working with the first stage of containment, she visualizes her overwhelming rage as "a huge orange and red sun." (This gives the feeling a shape and a color.) As she sits with that image she lets all of the rage magically and safely get absorbed into the sun. Next, she imagines putting the sun into another container to heighten the sense of safe storage: she sees it going into a large wooden asbestos box with a carved lid to keep it inside. Again, she sits with the imagery to make sure it is effective. If Maria says the rage feels "somewhat," "sort of," or "almost" contained she is invited to add more layers. She puts "a red and grey fireproof blanket made of scratchy wool" over the box, then "heavy black chains over the blanket" and finally, "glittery, soft, silver angel wings over the whole thing." At this point her body feels relaxed and comfortable, and she reports that a sense of genuine containment has been achieved.

Notice how her descriptions of containers captured color, texture, and size. The more you add the five senses to the imagery, the more vividly you will see it and the more deeply it will be installed. Really give yourself permission to take time with this so the imagery is detailed and authentic for you. It's also important to notice your non-verbal responses during this process. Ideally, you are looking for slower breathing, softening of the muscles in your face and body, and a release of overall tension. This indicates that safety is being achieved and the imagery is working for you.

Once the emotion is contained, you can choose to re-visit it during the course of the week. Or you can keep it contained until you are back in the safety of a therapist's office or you're able to get guidance from an equally comforting resource. To ensure that material won't "leak out" of its containers, you can put everything into an imagined bank vault with a timer that doesn't allow it to be re-opened until you decide that it's safe to re-visit it. This heightens your sense of control and provides reassurance that you can go about your daily life without the intrusion of upsetting emotions. Ultimately, it teaches you that there are strategies other than using self-destructive behaviors or burying feelings that you can turn to when trying to manage emotions.

Visualization Exercise: Imagining internal containers to store overwhelming emotions

Find a safe and comfortable place where you will be undisturbed for approximately 15 minutes. You can set a timer if you need an external way to be regrounded. Then follow the simple steps below:

1) choose an emotion to "target" (you might want to revisit one of the emotions you identified in an earlier journal entry when you explored the "negative affect" part of the cycle).
2) use your hands to make a gesture of "gathering it all up," then see, in your mind's eye, that the emotion is being contained by letting it get absorbed into a shape and a color.
3) think about a "container" where you can store the shape and color.
4) imagine placing the representation of your emotion into that first container.
5) sit with that image for a few moments and see if the emotion feels *fully* contained for you. If not, strengthen the imagery of the first container in some way (make the color more vivid or the shape bigger), or put the first container into a second, larger container so it strengthens the storage of your emotion (such as putting a blanket over a box, or burying one container in sand).
6) sit with that second layer of containment. Look for the body cues that signal a sense of safety and calm, including slower breathing and a softening of muscles.
7) add as many additional layers of containment as you need to fully accomplish that state of calm. If needed, put everything into a timed vault or any other image that guarantees relief from the emotion until you choose to re-visit it.

You can heighten your imagery by drawing or collaging it as well. By definition, putting images down on paper is a form of containment since overwhelming emotion stays within the boundary of the page. Once you've come up with a visual image for the container, take a picture of it on your cellphone and also use it as a screen saver on your laptop. In this way, anytime you need a reminder about containing emotion you can simply look at your phone or computer!

VISUAL EXERCISE: DRAWING CONTAINERS FOR OVERWHELMING EMOTIONS:

You can also pair another useful visualization strategy with art to give yourself a greater sense of control over your emotions. This strategy involves a "color wheel or palette" and simple breathing. Start by choosing your targeted emotion, and imagine a color wheel with 10 sections. Think about your targeted feeling at its most intense (10 out of 10) and give it a color. Then think about that emotion as it begins to lose its intensity (going from 9 down to 0) and pair each number with slight changes in the color. For example, anger at "10" might be bright red, and at "0" might have turned into a soft pink. So, each number and shade of color represents the level of intensity of that emotion. Now draw the color wheel with segments numbered from 1 to 10 and add the corresponding shades of color below each number.

As you begin the process of regulating your emotion, imagine placing a paintbrush on the number and color that represents the intensity of what you feel. Typically the starting point for rage, disappointment, or other scary feelings is between 7 and 10. You will now use your breathing to "move" the paintbrush to the next lower number and color on your wheel. First inhale, then exhale, letting your breath "control" the brush, moving it down as the feeling lessens. This is a creative form of biofeedback. It teaches you about the mind–body connection and your ability to "control" emotion through breath work. It also helps to notice what happens in your body as the upsetting feeling begins to lessen. The example below will help to clarify this strategy.

Forty-three-year-old Winona was grieving the profound loss of her infant in childbirth. Convinced that "her body killed the baby" she was punishing herself by withholding food. Her grief was all consuming and triggered a deep state of depression. Winona rated the intensity of her grief as a "10" and described it as "a dark midnight blue." If the intensity of her grief decreased to "0" the color would change until it became a "soothing aqua." Winona drew her wheel of 10 segments, with numbers corresponding to their matching shades of color. Then, she imagined putting the paintbrush on "10" and slowly began to breathe. Each exhale moved the brush down the palette. Sometimes, it took several breaths to move the brush and that's perfectly fine. Winona focused on the numbers decreasing and the color slowly changing with each breath. This gave her a concrete way to measure the shift in her emotional state. It also gave her back some control, as she could decide "how blue" she wanted to be in the present moment.

VISUALIZATION AND DRAWING EXERCISE: CREATING A COLOR WHEEL TO DECREASE OVERWHELMING EMOTION

Choose an emotion you'd like to decrease in intensity. Think about the color of that feeling at its highest intensity (10 out of 10), and then each changing shade as it decreases in intensity to a 0. Draw the color wheel below, then in your mind's eye place the paintbrush at the number representing it's current intensity. Now begin to slowly inhale and exhale, imagining that your breathing can move the paintbrush down the color wheel, until you get to 0 and the new, soothing shade.

Identify the distressing emotion _____ rate the intensity _____

(draw the segmented wheel with numbers above it, add the appropriate colors)

Identify the distressing emotion _____ rate the intensity _____
(draw the segmented wheel with numbers above it, add the appropriate colors)

Identify the distressing emotion _____ rate the intensity _____
(draw the segmented wheel with numbers above it, add the appropriate colors)

You can also use this strategy to increase the intensity of *desirable* emotions such as positive self-worth, confidence, or safety. In this instance the starting number is usually quite low and you can use your breathing and positive thoughts to move the paintbrush *upwards*. Notice how the color turns brighter or bolder as you tap into a stronger sense of your positive feeling.

When you practice this connection between a vivid color (such as gold) with a positive feeling (self-love) and an accompanying positive thought ("I am worthwhile") you can eventually just "go to the color gold" and feel the positive emotions, thoughts, and body sensations that have become associated with the color.

Identify the positive emotion _____ rate the intensity _____

(draw the segmented wheel with numbers above it, add the appropriate colors)

Identify the positive emotion _____ rate the intensity _____
(draw the segmented wheel with numbers above it, add the appropriate colors)

Identify the positive emotion _____ rate the intensity _____
(draw the segmented wheel with numbers above it, add the appropriate colors)

You can deepen this experience by finding an object, piece of fabric, or color chip from a paint wheel that matches the color you've been visualizing. This becomes another available resource to carry when you are looking to quickly increase a positive state of mind.

Another approach that has become quite popular and is extremely effective is the use of EFT or Emotional Freedom Technique. Created by Gary Craig, this deceptively simple "energy psychology" allows you to tap on specific acupressure points, helping to ease the flow of energy and reduce feelings of distress. There can also be additional benefit when this soothing self-touch is paired with a positive thought and an acknowledgment and acceptance of all emotions. When I teach my clients Tapping, I encourage them to do an alternating left and right touch, to help "wake up" the left and right hemispheres of the brain. This leads to a deeper integration of the experience. A great advantage to this strategy is that you can do it anytime and experience relief relatively quickly.

There are some excellent demonstrations on YouTube that give you Tapping scripts and show you specific places called "meridian points" on the hand, face, and body to tap. If you search for "EFT," "Gary Craig," or "tapping" (although you first might get a Fred Astaire dance routine!) you will find good resources. I have also found that the availability of so many videos invites a non-judgmental curiosity, and normalizes the use of EFT as a legitimate tool in managing emotions.

Behavioral Exercise: Practicing tapping for affect regulation

(You will need to check out the "how to" videos on-line before you practice so you can learn about the specific places on the body to tap)

1) Choose a targeted emotion—name it.

2) Rate the intensity from 0 to 10.

3) Notice where you feel the sensation on your body.

4) Begin the Tapping sequence (alternating left and right) as you pair it with the following sentence:

"Right now I feel (insert name of emotion or the positive affirmation) and I accept myself fully and completely".

5) Inhale and exhale.

6) Move to the next Tapping site and repeat.

7) Rest and then take a moment to rate the level of intensity again. If it is not lowered enough, repeat steps 3–6.

An additional tool that has been around for centuries and is getting newfound respect in the treatment of trauma, depression, anxiety, and self-destructive behaviors is yoga. There are many benefits to incorporating yoga into this part of the treatment cycle. For trauma survivors or anyone who uses dissociation, yogic breath work can be a relatively easy way to get quickly grounded and feel an immediate connection to the body, which increases a sense of safety. Practices like yoga, qigong and tai chi can offer you non-threatening ways to re-connect with body sensations, increase a state of mindfulness, and create a healthy sense of power and control. These experiences can profoundly influence your emotional states. Creating positive mind—body connections translates into feeling comforted, safe, energized, powerful, and serene.

Thirty-year-old Stan had been repeatedly physically abused in childhood by a trusted authority figure in his life. No one in his extended family recognized his trauma and he began using dissociation much of the time in order to survive his ongoing ordeal. As a result, in adulthood Stan was so disconnected from his body that he could run 26- or 50-mile marathons on a broken ankle or with pneumonia. Despite the fact that he took pride in these accomplishments and his ability to block out all pain, on some level he realized he was doing lasting damage to his body. Through therapy he realized he had been abusively pushing his body in response to internal feelings of guilt and shame about "not being strong enough to fight off his female abuser." Stan found the courage to begin doing simple yoga poses and discovered a new way to feel strong and present in his body. This immediately caused a positive shift in his depressed mood and feelings of helplessness and hopelessness. It also ended the cycle of subjecting his body to wrenching physical abuse.

As we explore a variety of treatment options to help address the "negative feelings" part of the cycle, the role of medication should not be minimized or ignored. Medication can be extremely effective in reducing PTSD symptoms, the frequency and seriousness of dissociation, depressed mood and numbing, agitation, rage, and aggressive impulses towards self and others.

Every major psychiatric organization and authoritative body recognizes the important role that medication can play in the treatment of depression and anxiety disorders. Engaging in the medication conversation often involves more than one discussion. It's understandable that you might initially feel confused or resistant. Part of your reaction might be connected to what I call "medication myths." You may have either heard about medication secondhand from friends or the Internet, or you may have had a brief and unsuccessful experience with medication in the past and assume the outcomes will be the same for you now.

Given the differences in power between you and other authority figures in your life (including a therapist), it is important that you don't feel bullied or forced into taking medication. Just as the decision to stop hurting yourself is in your arena, the decision to try medication needs to be yours, too. Having said that, it's important that you make this decision from an educated place. This means truly understanding the pros and cons once you are equipped with the objective facts.

It is a clinician or physician's ethical responsibility to bring up the subject of anti-depressants, drugs for anxiety, and mood stabilizers with you, and to make sure you fully understand the benefits before ruling out medication as a useful option.

You might view taking medication as a "weakness." This may be a learned value from family and friends who do not have an accurate understanding of medication and base their opinions on fear and misinformation. Take the time to consider why you have the attitudes about medication that you have and be open to the possibility that this mindset is not actually your own. Try to compare taking medication for improved mental health with taking medication for asthma, high blood pressure, or diabetes. In all likelihood, you would not judge someone for needing those medications, and would probably never call a person who uses an inhaler for asthma "weak." In fact, taking medication when you would benefit from it is actually a sign of strength. It says you care enough about yourself to improve the quality of your life. It is a *pro-active* step to better your life, reduce pain, and increase your overall functioning. Try to hold that compassionate view when you think about whether or not medication would be helpful.

Resistance to taking medication may also reflect a core survival belief that you have to do everything on your own without any assistance because nothing else can be counted on in life. If this thought applies to you this is an opportunity to revisit the difference between "then" and "now." Believing that you have to fend for yourself is accurate information about how it *used to be* in your life, but it is not related to your current life circumstances. In fact, agreeing to take medication to help stabilize your moods can have a healing effect by strengthening the idea that it's acceptable to get outside support and you don't have to handle the challenges of life alone.

One of the "medication myths" that surfaces for a lot of people is the fear that they will get addicted to an anti-depressant. It's important for you to know that anti-depressants are *not* addicting. In order for a substance to be addicting three things must be present: physical dependence, tolerance (requiring higher and higher doses to achieve the same effect), and withdrawal. Anti-depressants *do not* cause physical dependence, meaning you will not crave the medication. While you might initially need to increase your medication to find the best dose for maximum symptom relief, this is not due to the development of tolerance. And in most cases, when properly weaned, there are no significant withdrawal symptoms from anti-depressants.

Another "myth" is the notion that drugs will alter your thinking. The ironic truth is that anxiety, dissociation, trauma, and depression can profoundly alter your judgment, memory, focus, concentration, behavior, and the quality of your thoughts! The right medication can rebalance all of that so you are better able to make decisions from a place of sound judgment.

If you are uncertain because you have had unsuccessful experiences with medication in the past, re-visit what you used and be honest about how accurately you followed directions. It might be that the medication didn't work because it was taken for too short a period of time at a very low dose with no physician follow-up. If side effects were the reason you stopped taking the medication there are newer drugs with lower side effect profiles. Initial nuisance side effects like a headache or upset stomach often go away, and you will certainly never be "forced" to stay on medication that makes you feel uncomfortable.

It is possible that you are already on medication but still struggling with symptoms of depression or the draining effects of anxiety. If this is the case your medication needs to be re-evaluated by your prescribing physician. Getting a "response" from medication is not the same thing as getting to "remission" which is defined as the relief of *all* symptoms that gave you the diagnosis in the first place. That should always be the goal. Consider the strong possibility that you can dramatically improve if your physician considers changing the dose, changing the drug, or using a second drug for augmentation—or boosting the effect of the first drug. If you are working with a therapist, he or she can be your advocate by either empowering you to go back to your doctor or getting a signed release to discuss this directly with your physician.

Although you may be socially and culturally conditioned to "pull yourself up by your bootstraps" or "just grin and bear it," keep in mind that without a "medication safety net" you may have great difficulty remembering, processing, or integrating the work you are trying to do to move forward with your life. Medication is not a "cure-all." However, it is often the first step towards helping with mood swings, restoring good eating and sleeping habits, and allowing you to re-claim that glimmer of hope that makes future healing work even possible.

If you decide to try medication and your depression or anxiety disorder is straightforward, I suggest involving your primary care physician whenever possible. There are many advantages to this, including the fact that there is less of a stigma and it is more cost effective for you to see your family physician or internist. Primary care physicians are well trained in the recognition and treatment of depression and anxiety disorders, and many have extensive experience in the variety of drug options that can be effective. It is also a way to provide a streamlined, holistic approach to your mental health and medical care.

If you are a trauma survivor, you may avoid seeing a doctor for a pap smear, mammogram, birth control, colonoscopy, or prostate exam because those procedures are too physically triggering for you. It can be helpful to first schedule an office visit that does not include a physical exam. In this meeting you can share some of your history and explain the things that trigger you. This can help your physician be more sensitive to your needs and assist you in gaining some initial comfort and trust, which will make subsequent exams and procedures emotionally and physically safer for you. In addition to getting those preventative screenings and exams, you might also need to be connected to a physician to deal with addiction issues, or medical complications that come from cutting, burning, bingeing, purging, or restrictive eating. When a primary care doctor sees you for medication, you are also increasing the likelihood that your other medical needs will be addressed as well.

WRITTEN EXERCISE: PROCESSING YOUR FEELINGS ABOUT MEDICATION

Take a few minutes to think about your views regarding the possible use of medication in your treatment. Allow yourself to explore the pros and cons, and pay attention to whether or not these ideas are truly yours, or someone else's influence.

_____

_____

_____

_____

_____

_____

_____

_____

_____

_____

_____

_____

_____

_____

_____

_____

_____

_____

_____

23

ADDRESSING TENSION AND ANXIETY

If you are unable to short-circuit the "loop of negativity" you can work on addressing the part of the cycle that brings you to a state of heightened tension and anxiety. It might be helpful to first revisit the physiology of anxiety; how and where it manifests in the body. It's worth going back and reviewing your journal entries about what you experienced in your body when you felt anxious. Anxiety is typically experienced through heart palpitations or heaviness on the chest, sweaty palms, dry mouth, a feeling of dizziness, a constricted or collapsed body posture, nausea or stomach upset, thought racing, and other symptoms of agitated movement. Identifying the "physical red flags" of anxiety is the first step towards being able to address them. The treatment for anxiety often starts with your ability to accurately label what's happening as "feeling anxiety or panic" rather than thinking you are "going crazy" or having a heart attack.

Once you understand the sensations as anxiety-based you can use strategies designed to treat these symptoms by helping you achieve a more relaxed state. You might benefit from techniques that involve breath work since anxiety is connected to a fight/flight response and is experienced in the body. Controlled, conscious breathing is a great way to re-balance an overly activated system. Simple, rhythmic breathing seems to work best as it is easiest to master and can quickly re-connect you to your body.

Make sure you fully exhale. If you are a trauma survivor or grew up in a chaotic or dysfunctional family you may have a history of holding your breath to "listen" better when checking out the safety of an environment, the mood of a caretaker, or as the normal part of a freeze response. Holding the breath, or quick, shallow breathing actually increases a state of tension in the body. There are some wonderful breathing exercises that can be borrowed from practices such as "sun breath" in the yoga tradition, mindfulness, and Buddhist meditation. Here are a few "scripts" that can either be incorporated into a therapy session, or used on your own when you reach this stage in the cycle. In all cases, it helps for you to have both feet firmly on the ground and to be sitting in an upright but comfortable position so your diaphragm can be fully open to help you breathe properly.

> Fourteen-year-old Fran was frequently affected by "anticipatory anxiety" in response to being teased by peers. This meant she assumed her interactions with schoolmates would be painful and, as a result, got anxious just thinking about future encounters with them. Since she couldn't always control her environment, we worked on reducing her anxious state by helping her achieve a greater sense of internal safety—which was in her control. In session we practiced inhaling through the nose while slowly counting to 3. Fran then held her breath for 3 counts, and slowly exhaled through her nose for 5 counts. The additional counts when she exhaled allowed her to fully release the breath. In the next breathing set she was encouraged to pair inhaling with a soothing word—she chose to say the word "calm" in her mind. Then when she exhaled she chose the word "safe." She liked this strategy because the words brought up positive images in her mind. This helped her body to "slow down" in response to the breathing and reduced the agitation she felt from her anxiety.

Amy Weintraub, the founder of LifeForce Yoga for Mood Management, describes a wonderfully empowering exercise that incorporates a yogic pose and breath work. Begin by standing with your feet firmly planted in "Mountain Pose." As you inhale, imagine the breath traveling up through the crown of your head as you silently say the words, "I am." As you exhale, visualize the breath flowing downward, through your feet, as you silently say "here." A few rounds of this can help you to feel more centered, powerful, and present.

Another simple strategy is to place your arms, palms up and hands open, in your lap. As you inhale, let your fingers slowly close, and then slowly re-open them as you exhale. Matching the rhythm of breathing to the opening and closing of your hands helps you to slow down your breathing while focusing on your body in a way that creates a state of calmness.

You can also learn to incorporate hand-in-hand meditation, a Buddhist form of breath work designed to enhance mindfulness and reduce anxiety. Starting with both hands, palms up, in your lap, put one hand on top of the other and simply "notice" the sensation of one hand in the other hand. These sensations include: any difference in weight between the right and left hand; difference in the warmth or coolness of each hand; an awareness of air traveling between the hands, fingers, and on top of the palms. This heightened awareness of sensations on your hands can then be transferred to the breath: noticing the difference between breathing in and breathing out. You can then switch back and forth between an awareness of the hands and your breathing. In addition to its calming effect, this meditation gives you a healthier way to feel a sense of control and mastery over your body.

An Ericksonian approach invites you to simply observe the difference between inhaling and exhaling. Each time you breathe in and out, notice the sensations in your stomach, across your chest, along the tops of your shoulders, or inside your nose. This can heighten a sense of awareness, focus, and calm. Notice the shifts that breathing creates in your body: expanding and releasing; rising and falling; tensing and letting go.

If you feel like it's impossible to "take a breath," Amy Weintraub suggests in *Yoga for Depression* slowly singing E-I-E-I-O from "Old MacDonald Had a Farm." Or spend a minute slowly blowing soap bubbles. This forces you to breathe without really thinking about it!

BEHAVIORAL AND WRITTEN EXERCISE: PRACTICING MEDITATIVE BREATHING

Find a comfortable, private location and focus on any sensations of tension or anxiety in your body. Rate the level of intensity. Then choose one of the strategies described above and practice. When you're done, rate the level of tension in your body (0 = none, 10 = highest). In a few minutes, try another strategy (again rating the intensity of tension or anxiety before and after the breath work.) The advantage to practicing more than one technique is that it gives you more tools in your toolbox! Now take a few moments and write down your thoughts about these exercises.

1) Breathing strategy: _____

   Level of anxiety/tension BEFORE breath work: _____

   Level of anxiety/tension AFTER the breath work: _____

   My feelings about using the strategy: _____

   _____

2) Breathing strategy: _____

   Level of anxiety/tension BEFORE breath work: _____

   Level of anxiety/tension AFTER the breath work: _____

   My feelings about using the strategy: _____

   _____

3) Breathing strategy: _____

   Level of anxiety/tension BEFORE breath work: _____

   Level of anxiety/tension AFTER the breath work: _____

   My feelings about using the strategy: _____

   _____

The advantage to using breath work is that it is always available to you. However, it is possible that you have felt self-conscious about your breathing, as anxiety can quicken it and make inhaling and exhaling uncomfortable. In these instances, using art, visualization, and guided imagery can be quite helpful. Using line, shape, and color to visually show the depth, rate, and speed of inhaling and exhaling can be a safe way for you to connect to your breathing. You can also begin to play with the idea of taking more control over your breathing by deliberately drawing more slowly, using soothing colors, and making the lines on the page more expanded and fluid. This becomes a creative form of "biofeedback" and teaches you about the power of the mind–body connection.

DRAWING EXERCISE: USING LINE, SHAPE, AND COLOR TO DOCUMENT BREATH

If it still feels difficult to slow down your breathing, you can use drawing to simply release the energy and over-arousal that you do feel. You can illustrate your heightened state by choosing the appropriate colors and then scribbling or making staccato marks on paper with magic markers or colored pencils. Using these media rather than paints or pastels will help to keep the imagery more contained. As your experience is validated, it will actually begin to calm you down. You can then attempt to shift the imagery and the pace of your drawing so your breathing becomes slower and deeper.

DRAWING EXERCISE: DISCHARGING TENSION WITH ART

Choose colors that represent your anxious or tense state and simply scribble with one or both hands to release what you feel

Much of the early groundbreaking work that was done in the treatment of anxiety and panic emphasized the idea of "floating" with the thoughts and body sensations that accompanied anxiety, rather than "fighting" against them. Dr. Claire Weekes was one of the earliest advocates of this model. The idea of *going with* anxiety or panic may seem counter-intuitive to you, especially if your primary way of coping involves immediately disconnecting from feelings or fighting against upsetting thoughts. However, fighting the sensations by tensing the body or verbally bullying yourself actually heightens an anxious state and prolongs the experience.

Instead, you can learn to work with anxiety by pairing it with a visual image of floating. As always, you need to think of imagery that works for you, but some effective suggestions include: a balloon, a feather, or a cloud floating in the sky; a slow moving leaf or an empty canoe floating on a river. As mentioned when we discussed containment, the more vividly you can describe the imagery the more deeply you will connect to it. When you reach this stage of the self-destructive cycle, your growing anxiety can be stopped through this combination of mindful breathing and imagery that literally slows down your body.

WRITING AND GUIDED IMAGERY EXERCISE: FLOATING WITH ANXIETY/PANIC

Find a quiet, comfortable location. Think about an image that you connect with floating. Take a few moments and write down a detailed description then spend some time visualizing that image. Allow any thoughts or body sensations of tension or anxiety to "float" along with your image.

My image for floating:

_____

_____

_____

_____

_____

_____

_____

_____

_____

_____

_____

_____

_____

_____

_____

_____

_____

_____

Relaxation tapes or CDs can also be very helpful to you. In addition, sounds of nature, soothing music, or a calming voice can bring you to a more relaxed state. There are wonderful yoga nidra CDs that encourage you to focus on body sensation as a source of comfort, guiding you to a deeper state of relaxation and inner peace. I recommend that you preview tapes or CDs by listening to them in the store before buying them. This will ensure that there is nothing triggering about the music or the tone of voice.

You might also find it useful to read positive messages when your tension builds, as you can be soothed and calmed by reassuring thoughts of hope or faith. In addition to words that are spiritually based, learning that anxiety is time-limited and will always pass can also prevent such uncomfortable thoughts and feelings from increasing. Specific phrases can be used to quickly challenge distorted thoughts and re-ground you when you begin to feel your anxiety building. Helpful thoughts include: "Right now I am 'doing' anxiety or panic," "I know that in a few minutes my body will calm down," and "I can use my inner resources to help myself through this time-limited, uncomfortable feeling."

You can also use the same "color wheel and numbers" imagery described earlier to bring down your anxiety. Choose a color that represents the highest level of anxiety (10) and shift the color to one of total calm (0). Refer back to the section on working with negative emotions as a reminder of how to use this technique to work through your mounting tension.

DRAWING AND WRITING EXERCISE: REDUCING TENSION AND ANXIETY

Identify how/where you experience tension:

_____

_____

_____

_____

Rate the intensity: _____

(draw the segmented wheel with numbers above it, add the appropriate colors)

Identify how/where you experience tension:

_____

_____

_____

_____

Rate the intensity: _____

(draw the segmented wheel with numbers above it, add the appropriate colors)

Identify how/where you experience tension:

_____

_____

_____

_____

Rate the intensity: _____

(draw the segmented wheel with numbers above it, add the appropriate colors)

As is the case with other parts of the cycle, it's so important to choose strategies that feel safe, comfortable, and easy to do. If you half-heartedly agree to use techniques at different intervention sites, you will not experience much success and are at increased risk to go back to your self-destructive behaviors when you feel triggered or overwhelmed. Strategies that are reluctantly attempted and then fail reinforce the distorted idea that "nothing will help" and can cause you to lose faith in the process. Therefore, find the courage to be honest in your work and continue to monitor both your verbal and non-verbal responses to these suggestions. This will give you an accurate sense of what really feels comfortable for you. Remember you possess veto power to overrule any strategy you feel hesitant about doing! And remember, a strategy that doesn't feel right when you first try it can still be useful at a later time.

24

LEARNING TO STAY PRESENT

This is one of the most important parts of the cycle, as some degree of dissociation is typically needed in order for you to actually pick up the razor blade and cut more deeply than you intended, force excessive amounts of food into your body, "stand outside of yourself" and start drinking again, or keep rolling the dice when you are broke. As you learn to short-circuit this sensation, following through with destructive acts becomes much more difficult to do.

You must always remember that no one has the power to "take away" your ability to dissociate, nor should anyone attempt to do so. Even if anyone had that skill it's not the goal of treatment, as this would make you feel even more powerless. At this stage of the cycle, the goal is to help you understand and identify your dissociation and then allow you to either zone out, and "go to the ceiling," or to stay forward and grounded in the present. This concept of actively making decisions helps avoid a potential power struggle and reinforces the idea that *you do have choice and a sense of control over your behaviors.*

Just as we discussed the red flags that can indicate anxiety, you have physical cues that signal the onset of zoning out as well. Since it happens in such a knee-jerk way, perceived threat is instantly responded to with dissociation. Therefore, you need guidance to consciously re-connect to your dissociative experiences. If you are currently in therapy you might sometimes get "spacey" or zone out right in the middle of a session. This is especially true if you are discussing self-destructive behaviors! If that happens, see it as an opportunity and process the experience as it unfolds in the office. Ask yourself, "What just happened?" "Where did I just go?" See if you can describe what you were feeling in your body when you started to zone out. Look for experiences that include: a feeling of tunnel vision; seeing your therapist's mouth moving but not hearing what he or she is saying; feeling like a black curtain or black cloud is hovering over you or in front of your eyes; a tingling sensation in your arms and legs; a specific kind of headache; dizziness; a loss of body sensation or numbness; feeling disoriented or disconnected from the environment.

Of course, any of those dissociative sensations can happen in other situations and interactions with people, so pay attention to those experiences and ask the same questions. It will also help to re-visit your earlier journal entry where you wrote about the ways in which you personally relate to dissociation.

Once you can notice these sensations *as they are happening* you've increased awareness and created the opportunity to introduce the concept of *choice*. This can be accomplished by using the following strategy as a healthier tool for coping: "I feel myself starting to dissociate because I'm aware of those physical red flags. Is it in my best interest to check out, or would it be more empowering for me to stay forward in the present moment?" The most important part of that phrase relates to what is "more empowering" for you. Initially, this might be confusing if you have associated power and safety with zoning out to escape an overwhelming or threatening experience.

This intervention helps to shift your ideas about dissociation. The behavior that was life saving in the past is the very same strategy that puts you back into a "freeze" response and makes you helpless in the present. As we discussed before, when you are in a dissociative state you are essentially in the more primitive parts of your brain. This means the more evolved part of your brain, the pre-frontal cortex, is "off-line" and you are unable to use your abilities to analyze, reason, gain insight, or use good judgment. Therefore, you are not in the best position to self-protect or advocate for yourself. It may take time for you to accept that this "lifejacket" is actually harmful to your wellbeing. Once upon a time dissociation helped you cope and survive but now it keeps you helpless and stuck, and probably hijacks your everyday functioning.

Once you assess that staying forward is typically the desired way to serve your best interests, you will need guidance in learning how to avoid full-blown dissociation. The introduction of grounding strategies becomes an important intervention in this part of your work. There are a variety of simple techniques that can help you re-connect to the present. As you process these options and test them out you can see how effective they are, while working through any initial resistance or roadblocks. Sometimes *identifying* your dissociative state, *re-labeling* it as disempowering, and *giving yourself permission* to stay forward is all that is required to short-circuit the process. At other times, once you identify your dissociative state you will need the additional support of visual cues, physical movement, or body sensations that serve as reminders of being grounded.

Whenever 60-year-old Colette explored her childhood neglect she felt herself "zoning out" in session. Our first step was making sure she had both feet on the floor. Her dissociation usually caused her to collapse and constrict her body, moving into a fetal position to feel safer. We worked with this by getting her into a standing position, encouraging her to bend her knees and bounce a bit so she could feel herself rooted to the floor. Incorporating yoga positions such as "mountain pose" or "warrior pose" also enhanced her sense of being physically grounded. Sometimes, she would take off her shoes to feel her feet on the floor, or roll her feet over a foot massager. At other times it helped to do jumping jacks, stomp, rub her hands together vigorously, clap or snap her fingers. She also learned to put one hand on her belly and one on her heart, anchoring herself to the movement of breath and the rhythm of her heartbeat.

We can also introduce body sensations such as tapping with cupped hands along the outside of the body, putting cold water on the face, sucking on an ice cube, strong mint, or sour lemon candy, or holding a cup of warm coffee, tea, or hot chocolate to activate the senses of touch and smell. You can grab onto a piece of jewelry such as a wedding ring or bracelet from a loved one and pair it with thoughts of being safe. As we discussed earlier, car keys are terrific for re-grounding as they represent being empowered and not trapped. As simplistic as this may sound, these strategies can quickly bring you back into your body and your current environment. When you are "zoning out," you are often only able to do the easiest strategies.

In addition to the suggestions described above, when you dissociate during a therapy session or when you are in the company of people you trust you can use a movement therapy technique of mirroring back simple "hand and sound calls." You can encourage your therapist, or a trusted significant other, to start with very easy patterns such as clapping twice and slapping the thighs once. Your job is to watch, listen, and repeat the movement sequence. This helps you to attend to the present moment, gets the more "thinking" part of your brain back "on-line," and de-rails your ability to "zone out." The "calls" can gradually become more complicated by combining clapping, snapping, placing arms across the chest, or tapping the toes.

When you begin to dissociate there is also an increased vulnerability for flashbacks. As we discussed in an earlier chapter, flashbacks can be experienced in a variety of ways. Although most people typically associate flashbacks with visual images, you've learned that they can also be experienced viscerally, which means through body pain, nausea, dizziness, or other physical symptoms. There are also "cognitive flashbacks" which are thoughts rooted in the past that get misinterpreted as information about the present, such as "I am helpless" or "It will never get better." And flashbacks can be experienced emotionally, often through feelings such as terror, despair, and rage.

Since flashbacks instantly make you "travel back in time" and re-live deeply upsetting parts of your past trauma, it makes sense that you would perform self-destructive behaviors to quickly numb, distract, and short-circuit these overwhelming sensations. When you struggle with PTSD you can relive the past with such vivid intensity that it really seems as if the experience was happening all over again. This can leave you feeling helpless, terrified, age regressed, and completely alone. Therefore, helping you to better manage your dissociation and flashbacks is an essential part of the treatment process. This can be accomplished by teaching you a few flashback-halting exercises that can be practiced either with a therapist or on your own.

Many trauma experts agree that when you are in a flashback it's important to get grounded as quickly as possible by naming the memories without deepening or dwelling on them. This means, acknowledging your experience without pulling up any specific details. The goal is to come back to the present as quickly as possible. Otherwise, the memories can overwhelm your thoughts and feelings and keep you stuck in the past. This is not to say that describing and working through the details of past trauma is a bad idea. It's just that you don't want to focus on painful trauma while you are in the middle of a flashback!

Here is a simple way to both acknowledge the sensations of a flashback and then quickly re-orient back to the present time. You can use this little "script" as a way to re-ground when you start to feel the beginning of a flashback experience. In addition to filling in the responses in this workbook, you can carry the sentences with you on a neon index card or Post-it, so you have it with you wherever you go. This strategy allows you to label the flashback experience, and is a reminder that if you feel younger than your actual age you are in flashback mode. The script also encourages you to re-frame the experience as something that can be useful rather than something to fear, which begins to take some of the power away from it. Additionally, the script introduces the concept of "dual awareness" which reminds you that despite the intensity of your experience, in reality you are grounded in the present, which, unlike the past, is safe and empowering.

FLASHBACK-HALTING PROTOCOL

As I experience this <u>image/thought/feeling/or body sensation</u> I realize that I feel
_____ years old.

    This tells me that I am having a <u>visual, cognitive, emotional, or somatic</u>
flashback.

I am being given information back about how I used to <u>think/feel</u> in the past.
In the present, I can use this information to grow and heal.
In the present I can access support—I am not alone.

> Seventy-two-year-old Anthony had been held hostage by flashbacks for most of his life. Never understanding their root cause and always feeling powerless when they occurred, he stumbled upon the strategy of "spending 10 hours a day playing video games, as a way to distract my mind and keep the demons away." Using this simple flashback-halting technique gave him a newfound sense of control and reduced the need to self-medicate through his computer addiction. By filling in the blanks for each statement, he came to realize that feelings of being trapped and afraid, "seeing" his childhood basement, and the body sensation of intense stomach pain were emotional, visual, and somatic flashbacks about being hurt when he was eight years old. He experienced a breakthrough in treatment when he began to work with childhood pictures of himself and to re-connect with and comfort his hurt inner child.

BEHAVIORAL AND WRITTEN EXERCISE: FLASHBACK-HALTING PROTOCOL #1

It's ok to fill this in either right before you go into flashback, or after the fact.

A1) Image, thought, feeling, or body sensation:

_____

2)   Age I feel when I am in this state: _____

3)   Kind of flashback I am having (circle all that apply):

    VISUAL   EMOTIONAL   COGNITIVE   SOMATIC

4)   The information I am being given back about the past (circle all that apply):

    SOMETHING I SAW   SOMETHING I FELT IN MY BODY
    SOMETHING I HEARD   SOMETHING I THOUGHT
    EMOTIONS I FELT   SOMETHING I EXPERIENCED

5) How I can use this information to grow and heal:

_____

_____

_____

_____

6) How I can access support or comfort in the present:

_____

_____

_____

_____

B1) Image, thought, feeling, or body sensation:

_____

2) Age I feel when I am in this state: _____

3) Kind of flashback I am having (circle all that apply):

VISUAL   EMOTIONAL   COGNITIVE   SOMATIC

4) The information I am being given back about the past (circle all that apply):

SOMETHING I SAW   SOMETHING I FELT IN MY BODY
SOMETHING I HEARD   SOMETHING I THOUGHT
EMOTIONS I FELT   SOMETHING I EXPERIENCED

5) How I can use this information to grow and heal:

_____

_____

_____

_____

6) How I can access support or comfort in the present:

_____

_____

_____

_____

C1) Image, thought, feeling, or body sensation:

_____

2) Age I feel when I am in this state: _____

3) Kind of flashback I am having (circle all that apply):

VISUAL   EMOTIONAL   COGNITIVE   SOMATIC

4) The information I am being given back about the past (circle all that apply):

SOMETHING I SAW   SOMETHING I FELT IN MY BODY
SOMETHING I HEARD   SOMETHING I THOUGHT
EMOTIONS I FELT   SOMETHING I EXPERIENCED

5) How I can use this information to grow and heal:

_____

_____

_____

_____

6) How I can access support or comfort in the present:

_____

_____

_____

_____

If you are working with a therapist, practicing the use of this script during sessions helps to strengthen it as a resource for you when you are not in their office. Even if you are not currently in treatment, you can use this strategy as a way to re-ground yourself when you start to feel the signs of dissociating or going into a flashback state.

Another simple and effective strategy that is based on Milton Erickson's work with self-hypnosis can be used as a flashback-halting protocol. It will help you re-connect with your present environment. When you start to feel triggered and "spacey" say out loud, in sequence, five things you see, five things you hear, and five things you feel emotionally or in your body. Then go back to the beginning and say four of each, three of each, two and one of each. You can also do this as a written exercise. It's ok if you repeat what you've already said or written, and it's ok if you forget the order—there's no wrong way to do it! The idea is, you are re-directing your focus back to your current surroundings: a critical part of re-grounding and mindfulness awareness and a good way to short-circuit a flashback!

BEHAVIORAL AND WRITTEN EXERCISE: FLASHBACK-HALTING PROTOCOL #2

1) Five things that I see in my present surroundings:

_____

_____

_____

_____

_____

Five things that I hear in my present surroundings:

_____

_____

_____

_____

_____

Five things that I feel emotionally or in my body:

_____

_____

_____

_____

_____

Four things that I see in my present surroundings:

_____

_____

_____

Four things that I hear in my present surroundings:

_____

_____

_____

_____

Four things that I feel emotionally or in my body:

_____

_____

_____

_____

Three things that I see in my present surroundings:

_____

_____

_____

Three things that I hear in my present surroundings:

_____

_____

_____

Three things that I feel emotionally or in my body:

_____

_____

_____

Two things that I see in my present surroundings:

_____

_____

Two things that I hear in my present surroundings:

_____

_____

Two things that I feel emotionally or in my body:

_____

_____

One thing that I see in my present surroundings:

_____

One thing that I hear in my present surroundings:

_____

One thing that I feel emotionally or in my body:

_____

2) Five things that I see in my present surroundings:

_____

_____

_____

_____

_____

Five things that I hear in my present surroundings:

_____

_____

_____

_____

_____

Five things that I feel emotionally or in my body:

_____

_____

_____

_____

_____

Four things that I see in my present surroundings:

_____

_____

_____

_____

Four things that I hear in my present surroundings:

_____

_____

_____

_____

Four things that I feel emotionally or in my body:

_____

_____

_____

_____

Three things that I see in my present surroundings:

_____

_____

_____

Three things that I hear in my present surroundings:

_____

_____

_____

Three things that I feel emotionally or in my body:

_____

_____

_____

Two things that I see in my present surroundings:

_____

_____

Two things that I hear in my present surroundings:

_____

_____

Two things that I feel emotionally or in my body:

_____

_____

One thing that I see in my present surroundings:

_____

One thing that I hear in my present surroundings:

_____

One thing that I feel emotionally or in my body:

_____

25

USING CARESS

In an earlier chapter, you read about the idea of creating alternative "lifejackets" to give you strategies that provide the same, yet healthier, positive outcomes that you get from your self-destructive behaviors. As we discussed earlier, I strongly believe that "standard safety contracts" can often make the problem worse. Asking you to just stop doing your destructive behaviors often backfires. Hospitalization, although necessary when you are not stable and become a true danger to yourself, should be considered a last resort. It is important to remember that if you have harmed your body in a way that could be seriously damaging or dangerous, you probably require medical attention from an emergency room, and should seek it out. For long-term care, there is no real evidence that hospitalization is better than outpatient treatment when trying to manage self-destructive behaviors unless you are truly suicidal.

A better way to intervene at this part of the cycle is to incorporate the strategy of CARESS—Communicate Alternatively, Release Endorphins, and Self-Soothe. As we have already discussed, CARESS is an alternative to standard safety contracts that eliminates the power struggle between you and the people in your life who want you to stop hurting yourself. CARESS is specifically designed to help you achieve, in healthier ways, the same positive gains you get from self-destructive behaviors. You already know that self-destructive behaviors temporarily lessen tension and anxiety, and keep the re-surfacing of painful memories and emotions out of your reach.

It's equally important to remember that self-harm is a form of "meta-communication" (sharing information through actions rather than words) and the destructive behaviors represent your pain stories. When you target this part of the cycle focus on the dynamics of meta-communication. Remember to think about the behavior as an attempt to re-enact something painful, and then re-story or change the outcome of that prior traumatic experience. CARESS allows you to share your pain more productively. It also gives you creative ways to short-circuit uncomfortable emotions while helping you to feel soothed and calmer.

As an aside, although I have never encountered this personally in my work, it is worth stating that you might feel triggered by the word "CARESS." By definition, it means an embracing, soft touch, which is something I want you to feel comfortable offering yourself. It is meant to be a loving alternative to self-punishment. However, if the word means something unsafe to you, particularly if you are a sexual abuse survivor, you can modify the exercise to stand for "CARES" and still maintain all three essential parts.

As we have already discussed, when you initially become triggered it is impossible to think in rational ways. Therefore, when the urge to cut, purge, or drink kicks in, it is unreasonable to expect you will have the ability to turn to healthier coping strategies. With this in mind, it is helpful to start off by creating a CARESS box that will be kept in a safe place at home. (If you are working with a therapist, this is a great exercise to do in their office and then take home with you after session.) The box is used as a "container," holding all the tools that will be needed to effectively use CARESS when the self-destructive impulse strikes. This increases the likelihood that you will follow through with the strategies if everything is in one place and you don't have to frantically search for your resources when you feel the urge to hurt yourself.

To increase your emotional connection to the process and to personalize it, paint, collage, or draw words and images on the box that represent feeling safe, comforted, and soothed. Allow this project to unfold over time. If you are not doing this under the guidance of a therapist, make sure the words, images, and colors that you choose really bring up a calming response and don't trigger you in any way. If you are working with a clinician, they will be able to help you figure out whether or not your choices are calming or too stimulating for you. Eventually, this box will contain the resources that will help you walk through the rest of the CARESS protocol.

As you have learned, when you reach this stage of the cycle you are either intensely hypo-aroused (frozen and dissociative) or shifting into hyper-arousal (fight/flight) as you consider doing something self-destructive. We now understand that in either of those states, you are at a grave disadvantage and your capacity to think clearly about acts of self-care become compromised. Therefore, the first real step in treating acts of self-harm is to get re-grounded and present. To this end, before you can move ahead with the rest of the protocol, the first "C" in CARESS could also stand for "Centering."

There are many strategies that can assist you in re-connecting with the present moment, and you should try to practice them either in session with your therapist, or on your own, to help get some beginning mastery. This, in turn, will enable you to take greater advantage of the benefits of the CARESS model. Some of these ideas have already been identified as interventions that can be used when addressing the dissociative/numbing part of the cycle. You can use them here, as well.

Experiment with the following strategies to achieve a more "centered" state before moving into CARESS: simple breathing exercises while focusing on the sensations of inhaling and exhaling in the body; stating out loud what you see, hear, and feel in your current environment; using simple re-grounding phrases to bring you back into the present; using Tapping, yoga poses, and other simple movements to re-connect with the body; identifying your present location and age. It will not always be possible for you to start from a more centered place, but don't become discouraged. In many cases "going to the CARESS box" is the conditioned thought and behavior that begins the centering process for you!

Once you have worked on the concept of centering and you have personalized the box, you can begin to process the three stages of CARESS. Keep in mind this is not about asking you to refrain from your self-destructive behaviors. Rather, when you get the urge to act out, *before* you do, you will *first* use the strategies from CARESS. In this way we are trying to re-train your brain to associate the impulse to harm with an automatic CARESS response, rather than your conditioned self-destructive one. CARESS is presented as an alternative option to the coping strategies you've been using. The decision to utilize it is always up to you!

As you set the stage for CARESS, let's add the use of a timer. This can be an alarm on a clock, cell phone, oven, or egg timer. Each phase of CARESS is deliberately limited to 10–15 minutes so you never become flooded or overwhelmed by the strategy. Since you will often be doing CARESS by yourself, the sound of the timer becomes an external resource for boundaries and re-grounding, and reassures that you will not become "lost" in the work.

You should set the timer at the start of each CARESS section. When it goes off, you can either move on to the next phase of the work or re-set the timer for one more cycle. At the end of the second cycle, however, you are encouraged to move on to the next step. You are less likely to do your self-destructive behavior when you can successfully work with all three phases. After you see what the exercise looks like, I will walk you through an explanation of each part. This way, you will understand the rationale behind each step and will be more likely to try all three components. The actual "exercise" is as follows:

C.A.R.E.S.S.

I agree that when I get the impulse to self-harm, BEFORE I do, I will choose to do one behavior from each category below. (Set a timer so you have an external boundary to re-ground you after 10–15 minutes.)

C.A.—Communicate Alternatively (10–15 minutes)

Hurting the body is a way to communicate feelings, thoughts, needs, and unresolved trauma memories. Here are some ideas for other, less destructive ways to communicate.

- Draw/paint the body part and the injury you'd like to do—add words to the images
- Draw the emotions that go with the urge to do something self-destructive
- Make a collage of words/images that capture thoughts/feelings
- Describe what you feel by talking into your cellphone or a tape recorder
- Write a poem about your feelings
- Find the lyrics to a song that express what you are feeling
- Sculpt the body part with clay and use your fingernail to show the injury

- Write a detailed description of doing your self-harming behavior
- Send yourself an e-mail about what was happening when wanting to self-harm

R.E.—Release Endorphins (10–15 minutes)

You feel better after you self-harm because the brain releases endorphins (naturally occurring pain killers) in response to pain/body trauma. Here are other ways to experience the release of endorphins:

- Run up/down the stairs or around the outside of your house/march in place
- Do 100 jumping jacks
- Workout on exercise equipment
- Do a part of an at-home exercise tape/put on the radio and dance
- Listen to a funny comedian on a CD/video
- Watch a funny movie/TV show
- Watch a YouTube video of a baby laughing or silly pet tricks
- Read something that tickles you
- Hold/stroke and hug a stuffed animal or live pet
- Hug a pillow, rag doll, or a tree

S.S.—Self-Soothe (10–15 minutes)

You deserve to learn new strategies that promote self-care and decrease anxiety from future triggering events. Here are some additional ways to be comforted.

- Wrap yourself in a quilt and rock in a rocking chair
- Take a warm shower/bubble bath
- Light scented candles or oil
- Read positive affirmations or something spiritual
- Massage your hands with soothing lotion
- Listen to a relaxation tape/play soothing music
- Slowly blow bubbles to slow down breathing
- Call a 24-hour hotline to hear a comforting voice

Now let's explore CARESS in more detail, so you fully understand its benefits.

CA: COMMUNICATE ALTERNATIVELY

This gives you another way to "show" the story of your pain so it can be witnessed, discussed, and eventually healed. The use of right-brain-based creative techniques is important because trauma memories are not stored in the part of the brain that handles language (Broca's area). This means traumatized people often don't have words to describe their experiences. In addition, if you were abused, your perpetrator's threats against "telling" may make it impossible for you to talk about your pain. Therefore, you need other ways to communicate your experiences, accessing them with the help of strategies that bring information forward from the more primitive parts of the brain.

You get to choose which communication strategies feel safest and most comfortable for you since the CARESS model supports the idea of helping you keep a sense of control. The options are designed to bring together both right and left hemispheres of the brain, as this will enable you to best process and work through the material. As you select the strategies, it helps to write down your choices in the workbook (see exercise below) as well as on a brightly colored index card or Post-it note. This can be placed in the CARESS box as a kind of "cheat sheet" or reminder since it is understood that it's more difficult to think clearly when you are triggered.

One strategy for "CA" uses art therapy techniques to help you re-channel harmful urges. You can draw or collage the body part you want to injure, along with a visual display of the injuries. You can also mold the body part out of clay and then use your fingernail to show the injuries. This safely and effectively helps you to "show" the pain and emotion that you have probably been illustrating on your body through cutting, burning, bruising, eating disordered behaviors, drugging, drinking, or unsafe sexual activities.

You can draw, paint, or collage the "words" and "feelings" you vomit when purging or shove back down when bingeing, or the emotions that go with the desire to drink, drug, starve, gamble compulsively, or sexually act out. This becomes a way for you to non-verbally express and de-code the deeper emotional expression of these behaviors. You may feel understandably nervous about writing or drawing your self-destructive behaviors or intense feelings, fearing this will cause an increase in the behaviors. But I have found that helping you "show" your pain and communicate your needs and feelings dramatically reduces the desire to actually do the behavior. Keep in mind that one of your primary goals is to "tell" your story and have it witnessed, and art therapy techniques allow you to safely do that.

Although you are encouraged to use these artistic techniques when you are using CARESS on your own, these are strategies that can also be woven into therapy sessions. You may, in fact, get the urge to self-harm in your therapist's office, particularly when you are talking about things that are emotionally charged or threatening. Perhaps you use innocent but sharp objects like pens, pencils, paper clips, or fingernails pressed into the palm of a hand, nail biting, or hair pulling. You are not alone in this behavior, and it makes sense that sometimes you will want to "distract" or "disconnect" from a difficult session. However, when this occurs try to recognize that it is an opportunity to practice using artwork or writing in the session to communicate your feelings in another, healthier way.

You'll know if you are in the right clinical hands if your therapist encourages this rather than ignoring what you are doing or shaming you for it. A therapist who understands this model will offer you paper, markers, crayons, or colored pencils and direct you to "draw" what you are thinking, feeling, or wanting to do on your body. Koosh balls with elastic strings that can be tugged, or a variety of foam or squishy "squeeze" toys can also be used as alternatives to self-harm if you don't feel like drawing. The idea is to get the behavior "off of the body." If your therapist is trained in sand narrative work and has a sand tray in their office this can be another extremely useful way to help you communicate and process the deeper meaning of your actions.

If you have "performance anxiety" about using art, you can journal, write a poem or song lyric, send yourself an e-mail, or simply talk into a tape recorder, mini Dictaphone, or leave yourself a message on your voicemail. Regardless of the strategy, the idea is for you to freely express your thoughts and emotions about what you feel compelled to do, or provide additional information about your self-destructive behavior. When you are able to safely communicate by creating something that can be witnessed and discussed—rather than getting high, purging, starving, gambling, or leaving a cut, bruise, or burn on your body—the cycle of helplessness and repeatedly being a victim is stopped and true healing can begin.

RE: RELEASE ENDORPHINS

The idea behind this phase of treatment is to offer you additional ways to stop overwhelmingly negative thoughts and feelings through the release of naturally occurring painkillers that get produced in the brain. Remember that the reinforcing part of self-destructive behaviors is the release of endorphins through self-mutilation, bingeing and purging, or the temporary "euphoria" you might get through substance abuse, gambling, compulsive shopping, or self-imposed starvation. Although our brains release endorphins in response to intense pain, we can also experience this pleasurable sensation through hugging, laughter, and a big burst of physical activity.

After the timer has gone off and you have had the opportunity to give a new kind of "voice" to your pain, moving to this phase of CARESS is a healthier way to deal with being upset. Once again, you get to decide which options you want to try. In this phase of treatment, you might like a combination of the three strategies, incorporating a few minutes of physical activity, laughter, and hugging.

If you want to release endorphins through movement make sure you are physically fit enough to engage in the activity. This is particularly important if you struggle with obesity, are medically compromised, or very under-weight. You should refrain from intense physical exertion if you are using it as an attempt to do "exercise bulimia," which is a form of purging that combines excessive exercise with a lack of sufficient calories. If exercise is a safe option, you can spend 10–15 minutes doing activities including: jumping jacks; running around the outside of your home; going up and down the stairs; using a treadmill; putting on music and dancing; following an exercise routine from a DVD; kick boxing or shadow boxing; playing a high impact "motion-control" video game system such as "Wii" or a controller-free motion gaming device like "Kinect."

When possible, the idea is to maintain a high level of exertion to feel the endorphin release. Extensive research has gone into studying the positive effects of exercise on mood. In addition to increasing a sense of power, heightening control over the body, as well as a feeling of competence, exercise gives us an endorphin "kick," which serves as a healthy distraction and has a positive impact on thoughts and feelings. The release of endorphins enables long distance runners to endure the grueling miles and discomfort of the race. This same concept holds true for trauma survivors.

The second option involves laughter, a surefire way to short-circuit upsetting emotions and thoughts. Although a mere smile can have a positive impact, the idea is to go for belly laughs. This can be accomplished in a number of creative ways. You can cue up a funny scene from your favorite movie or watch the stand-up routine of your favorite comedian. I have found that using YouTube videos is a great way to quickly start laughing while creating a healthy distraction. In addition to the treasure trove of TV and movie clips from the past, you can search for either "silly pet tricks" or "babies laughing." These videos typically make anyone laugh.

Once again, it is important to think about these options ahead of time. If you have unresolved issues related to abortion, miscarriage, infertility, the death of a child, or the loss or death of a pet, then the YouTube videos would not work well. However, if you decide there is nothing emotionally loaded or potentially triggering about the topics, given the way our brains work, watching a child dissolve into a fit of laughter will create the same response in you!

The third option, hugging, can either stand on its own or be incorporated into the other strategies. It is important to emphasize that it isn't about hugging another person. CARESS has to be workable when you are by yourself because typically you will be alone when the self-destructive impulse takes over. Wrapping yourself in a blanket and hugging a pillow or stuffed animal, holding a pet or a doll usually works. You might even like to hug trees! The idea is to release that surge of warmth that we feel when we wholeheartedly hug something. This is also a good opportunity to try the EMDR butterfly hug: placing the arms across the chest and alternating gentle taps on the upper forearms with the fingertips. You can also think about the idea of hugging your "inner child," by holding a soft pillow close to your body while visualizing that you're hugging your younger, innocent self. There are even heart shaped pillows you can purchase on-line that come equipped with the feel of a "beating heart" so you can really experience the sensation of holding an imaginary child or pet.

SS: SELF-SOOTHE

Once you have communicated and successfully short-circuited your negative thoughts and feelings the timer is re-set so the endpoint of your work is something self-soothing. You are probably unsure about how to do this in healthy ways since your primary strategy has been doing something self-destructive! Therefore, you may need input and suggestions from a therapist or a loved one about how to self-soothe appropriately. Again the emphasis is on activities that can be done on your own. You shouldn't have to wait for someone else to be available in order to feel better. This might initially feel foreign to you, since getting comforted in childhood really was riding on someone else being available to you.

Some of the activities that you can try might include: taking a warm shower or bubble bath; listening to soothing music; giving yourself a hand massage with your favorite smelling lotion; reading a book of positive affirmations, something spiritual or grounded in the 12 step movement; calling a hotline to talk to a trained, sensitive person; meditating; singing a lullaby to yourself; holding and drinking a warm cup of tea or cocoa; "nesting" in pillows and blankets; massaging your temples and wrists with a relaxing scent such as lavender; taking a short walk through a garden; lying on the grass and watching the clouds in the sky; listening to a guided imagery or relaxation tape; watching an inspiring video; or looking through a book of beautiful photography. Putting one hand on your heart and the other on your belly and gently rocking is another movement that is universally experienced as soothing.

It is quite possible that you will not easily buy into these options. This is because they are probably unfamiliar and new, not because they are invalid and won't be effective in time. Choose strategies that you have some curiosity about and trust that with practice and repetition these behaviors will begin to feel more comfortable.

Once you have decided upon several possible behaviors under each of the three categories make sure they are all written down on an index card. The last step is to gather all of the resources you will need to follow through with your choices. This might include: paper; markers; hand lotion; the URL for the video; a soft blanket; the CD of soothing music, or the phone number for the 24-hour hotline. All of the items should be placed in your CARESS box for easy access.

When you find the courage to try CARESS, it is important to assess what is working and what needs to be re-visited. You might take to it instantly, doing all three phases and quickly feeling a great reduction in self-destructive behaviors. Or you might initially hold back, doing only part of CARESS, or just think about it without putting it into practice. If you have told trusted people in your life that you are working with CARESS, their job is to be patient, supportive, and encouraging, not to pressure you about doing it. Be gentle with yourself. Try to reinforce the smallest baby steps you take towards new behavior, never shaming yourself when you don't follow through. If you keep exploring the strategies and begin to apply them they will work. Besides, even thinking about or imagining new behaviors can have a positive impact on your body and brain, so reward yourself for taking that meaningful first step.

I want to emphasize that there is something deliberately missing from the CARESS model, and that's *calling your therapist* when you get the impulse to hurt yourself. Many caring and well-meaning clinicians might encourage you to reach out to them when you want to self-harm or are on the verge of relapsing. Although this is a kind gesture, I believe it can be a mistake. It gives you the subtle message that you *need* that therapist in order to be okay, which can lead to co-dependency. It also sets up a dangerous and unrealistic expectation about a therapist's availability and boundaries. A therapist cannot be on call 24/7 no matter how much they care about your wellbeing. You need to believe that you have what it takes to heal. CARESS reinforces the idea that everything you need to work through your issues exists inside of you. If you already have this established pattern of calling your therapist when you think about doing something self-destructive, allow yourself to take baby steps in the direction of waiting a longer period of time while trying other ways to soothe and calm yourself.

WRITTEN EXERCISE: USING CARESS

See if you can come up with a few ideas for CARESS, and then begin to find the resources and objects that you can put into your box for later use.

Three strategies I can use to communicate my thoughts and feelings (CA):

1) _____

2) _____

3) _____

Three strategies I can use to release endorphins (RE):

1) _____

2) _____

3) _____

Three strategies I can use to self-soothe (SS):

1) _____

2) _____

3) _____

List of objects I can use to accomplish my goals:

_____   _____

_____   _____

_____   _____

_____   _____

_____   _____

_____   _____

_____   _____

26

HONORING THE POSITIVE OUTCOMES

I am a strong believer that we don't continue to engage in a behavior unless we get something from it. This does not imply, in any way, that you like hurting yourself. It does infer, however, that what you do holds conscious or unconscious meaning, expectation, and assumptions. You might continue to do destructive behaviors to gain mastery, power, or control over something or someone. Other behaviors are repeated because the outcome, or "secondary gain" is pleasurable and gratifying. Frequently, behaviors are held on to because you hope the next time you engage in them something will finally change for the better. In any case, it is important to address this part of the cycle if you continually engage in self-destructive behaviors.

At times, you might be able to easily explain what your behaviors do for you, and you might understand how powerfully reinforcing the positive outcomes are, even if they are short-lived. At other times you might actually feel as if the behaviors "hold you hostage." You feel driven to engage in them almost against your will, and focus more on the after-effects of shame, guilt, and helplessness they create, rather than the short-term gains. When the positive motivation for engaging in your behaviors isn't clear, you are more likely to inaccurately see your actions as proof of your "craziness" or "weirdness."

The treatment of self-destructive behaviors typically focuses on why they are a problem and a bad idea. From a well-intended place, a helping professional might encourage you to focus on everything that is dysfunctional or wrong with your behaviors, hoping this will motivate you to stop. From your perspective, this can be experienced as disrespectful and humiliating, making you feel even "crazier." As a result, this may actually cause you to dig in your heels and cling even more tightly to your behaviors. When this occurs you are vulnerable to dropping out of treatment. You may legitimately feel anger towards your therapist because they "don't get it" and "don't get you," or why it makes sense in your mind to hurt yourself.

If instead you are given permission to explore and express the ways in which your self-harm "works" for you, shame is removed and the therapeutic relationship can deepen. When this is discussed in therapy you will believe your therapist understands that the behavior serves an important function and feels *necessary* to you. This does not mean the behavior is encouraged, or the fact that it may be creating serious issues for you is being ignored. However, it is important to acknowledge that for a *part* of you, the behavior is useful, and in all likelihood there is uncertainty, confusion, and conflict raging inside about whether or not to give it up. This inner conflict needs to be creatively explored in therapy. There are a number of strategies that can be effectively used. Borrowing from the work of Richard Schwartz, one step is to encourage you to connect with the "part" of you that feels the need to do the behavior. See if you can create a vivid description of that part. Think about how old it is, what it looks like, how it feels in your body, and how you feel when you access this part of yourself.

WRITING AND DRAWING EXERCISE: IDENTIFYING THE SELF-DESTRUCTIVE PART OF YOU

Find a quiet, safe place to begin thinking about the part of you that acts on your self-destructive urges. It's important to approach this part with compassion rather than anger or judgment. Now take some time to complete the following statements and then follow the drawing prompts when you are ready. This will help you gain an even greater understanding of your actions.

A1) I will be describing the part of me that engages in the following self-destructive behavior:

_____

_____

2) This part of me feels _____ years old.

3) When I visualize this part of me I see:

_____

_____

_____

_____

_____

_____

_____

_____

_____

_____

Draw the part that engages in the self-destructive behavior:

4) The adjectives I could use to describe the part that engages in my self-destructive behaviors might be:

_____   _____

_____   _____

_____   _____

_____   _____

_____   _____

5) The sensations I feel in my body when I access this part of me include:

_____   _____

_____   _____

_____   _____

_____   _____

_____   _____

The colors, shapes, and lines that illustrate those sensations might be:

6) The emotions I feel when I access this part of me include:

_____   _____

_____   _____

_____   _____

_____   _____

_____   _____

The colors, shapes, and lines that might express those emotions are:

7) I can have compassion for this part of me because:

_____

_____

_____

_____

_____

_____

_____

_____

8) Although this part causes me pain, I understand it may be trying to "protect" me by:

_____

_____

_____

_____

_____

_____

B1) I will be describing the part of me that engages in the following self-destructive behavior:

_____

_____

2) This part of me feels _____ years old.

3) When I visualize this part of me I see:

_____

_____

_____

_____

_____

_____

_____

_____

_____

_____

Draw the part that engages in the self-destructive behavior:

4) The adjectives I could use to describe the part that engages in my self-destructive behaviors might be:

_____   _____

_____   _____

_____   _____

_____   _____

_____   _____

5) The sensations I feel in my body when I access this part of me include:

_____   _____

_____   _____

_____   _____

_____   _____

_____   _____

The colors, shapes, and lines that illustrate those sensations might be:

6) The emotions I feel when I access this part of me include:

_____   _____

_____   _____

_____   _____

_____   _____

_____   _____

The colors, shapes, and lines that might express those emotions are:

7) I can have compassion for this part of me because:

_____

_____

_____

_____

_____

_____

_____

_____

8) Although this part causes me pain, I understand it may be trying to "protect" me by:

_____

_____

_____

_____

_____

_____

_____

Once the "self-destructive part" has been identified and you can feel some beginning compassion for it you can be encouraged to let this part "speak" through writing or drawing. Try writing with your non-dominant hand as this makes it harder to hide authentic emotions, thoughts, and memories. Two-handed writing can also be used by vertically dividing a piece of paper in half, posing non-judgmental questions on one side of the page using your dominant hand, then letting the self-destructive part respond on the other side of the page with your non-dominant hand. It's important that the questions are not posed in a threatening way. You'll need a compassionate invitation to have a "conversation" between parts that have been previously angry at or disconnected from one another.

Forty-year-old Harriet (H) illustrates the power of two-handed writing in this conversation with a self-destructive part of her (SD) that cuts and drinks. You can hear the initial conflict and resentment between the parts and then notice the shift into a kinder and more cooperative stance once the parts really begin listening to each other.

(H)   Why do you insist on cutting and making me drink?

(SD)   You NEED me! If I don't pick up the razorblade or get the alcohol in us then we're screwed. You don't get it!

(H)   I think that YOU don't get it. Whenever you cut me or get me drunk, people think I'm weird, and then I have to pick up the pieces to make it look good to the outside world.

(SD)   You think YOU have to hold it all together? I'm the one who keeps it together. Why don't you just back off?

(H)   Listen, I'm not stupid. If I back off then you take over. Don't you realize how hard my job is? I've got to keep you in check and try to prevent you from acting out.

(SD)   Maybe if you'd just let me numb you with cutting or booze then your job would get easier. Did you ever think of that? Just let me do my thing! Stop criticizing me for trying to keep us SAFE!!!!

(H)   When I let you do your thing, I get hurt.

(SD)   If you don't let me do my thing you'll be hurt even more!!

(H)   So now what do we do???

(SD)   You tell me!! You're the high and mighty expert around here.

(H)   Well, sometimes I don't want to be the expert!!

(SD)   Yeah, well sometimes I don't want to have to be the bad guy around here!

(H)   What do you mean? I thought you loved your job—creating excitement, making a mess.

(SD)   YOU'VE got the good job! You're the one with the answers, the one who makes the decisions, the one who everyone likes at work.

(H)   I'm tired. It's hard to keep it all together.

(SD)   I'm more tired! I'm the one with the razorblade. I know how much I scare you. I'm way more alone in here than you are.

(H)   This is weird. We BOTH feel alone and hated.

(SD)   It's really hard to be the one who does self-destructive stuff. Have you ever considered that?

(H)   Not till now. It's really hard to be me, too. I can't back down from you, I'm afraid of you.

(SD)   I'm trying to protect you from remembering stuff from the past or feeling the emotions that will overwhelm you.

(H)   Maybe there's other ways to feel protected. I guess I can appreciate what you're trying to do, but the truth is, I feel even more overwhelmed when my body gets hurt again, and that does bring back memories from the past.

(SD)   I didn't realize that hurting you reminds you of the past. But how else can we feel protected?

(H)   I'm not sure what the answer is yet—I'm just asking you to be open to letting me try something else.

(SD)   Ok.

WRITING EXERCISE: USING YOUR NON-DOMINANT HAND TO LET THE SELF-DESTRUCTIVE PART EXPRESS THE POSITIVE OUTCOMES

Use the space below to allow this part of you to explain the short-term positive outcomes of your destructive behaviors. This does not mean you "agree with" that part, or that you are encouraging it to continue, but rather it is an opportunity to fully understand it, so you can then work with it.

_____

_____

_____

_____

_____

_____

_____

_____

_____

_____

_____

_____

_____

_____

_____

_____

_____

_____

_____

WRITING EXERCISE: LETTING THE SELF-DESTRUCTIVE PART EXPRESS WHAT WILL BE "LOST" IF THE BEHAVIOR STOPS

Recognizing that you do these behaviors because you get something for them, use the space below to allow this part of you to express its worries, fears, or anxieties about what will be lost or what will change in your life if the self-destructive behaviors are no longer used.

_____

_____

_____

_____

_____

_____

_____

_____

_____

_____

_____

_____

_____

_____

_____

_____

_____

_____

_____

_____

_____

_____

WRITING EXERCISE: USING THE DOMINANT AND NON-DOMINANT HAND TO ENGAGE IN A "CONVERSATION" ABOUT THE BEHAVIOR—HOW IT HELPS AND HOW IT HURTS YOU

Using two different colored pens or pencils, write on one side of the page with one hand, then switch hands and colors and respond on the other side of the page with the other hand. The following is an example to help illustrate the exercise.

Why do you keep hurting my body? I actually feel so out of control.

Don't you get it? Hurting the body is the only way to actually be in control! Otherwise, you'd feel the rage from the past and that can really make us out of control.

But I feel guilty and afraid of myself. How is that "more in control?" There has to be a better way to deal with the rage. I feel like when I take it out on myself, I'm saying that my abusers in the past were right and I do deserve to be hurt!

I never thought of it that way. But unless you can come up with a better way to manage the rage, I feel like we have to keep cutting!

Ok. I'll keep working on it!

Now take a few sheets of paper, draw a line down the middle of each and explore your own conversation.

If you are working with a trained clinician, another effective tool taken from the Gestalt model of therapy is the "empty chair" technique. You can imagine the part that does the self-destructive or addictive behavior sitting in an empty chair and then engage in conversation with this part. Allow the "empty chair" to explain why the behavior feels necessary and what is at stake if it stops. Remember to process what will be *lost* if the behavior ends as this is just as important as understanding what is gained by doing it, and what will be gained by letting it go.

Take as much time as you need to fully explore these insights. It is so important to validate and "honor" the existence of this part. The longer-term goal is to shift from your initial reactions of shame, self-blame, and a desire to disown this part, to empathy, compassion, and acceptance. This is often accomplished when you start to think about this part's actions as "self-protective." This means exploring the ways in which seemingly destructive acts serve a "protective purpose."

Through your own insights as well as the support of professional guidance, you will see that your behaviors might "protect" by isolating you so intimacy is avoided. This, in turn, decreases the "risk" of being hurt or rejected. Sometimes "protection" is achieved through the numbing or distracting effects of your self-destructive behaviors. This keeps out the painful thoughts, feelings, and memories from the past. Of course, on a deeper level, it is a constant reminder of what happened, even if the conscious memory is not there. It is also protective in the sense that hurting the body is a way to "tell" without talking.

When a clinician allows you to explain the importance of your self-destructive behaviors it distinguishes that therapy from all of your prior therapy experiences, and this can bring hope into the room. It also enables you to gain more insight about the less conscious issues that drive and sustain the behaviors. Once you understand these insights, you feel less "crazy." Identifying positive outcomes is also a crucial intervention because it allows you to be curious about and explore other possible ways to achieve those same ends. Whether you need to feel protected from rejection, abandonment, failure, or intimacy, it can now be addressed in healthier ways. Once you understand the reinforcing power of endorphins, you become more willing to entertain other ways to get that same feeling of relief, such as trying CARESS.

It's also useful to address the "pay-off" of using self-harm to end an uncomfortable dissociative state, re-connect to your body, and feel re-integrated. Using some of the re-grounding strategies that help with dissociation can be applied to this part of the cycle as well. Working with the body to notice, create, and intensify physical gestures that feel empowering and freeing is a great way to help you safely re-connect to your body, without first making it experience pain.

Yoga poses and simple movement therapy techniques can provide you with healthier alternative ways to be "present" in your body, rather than relying on physical pain, the sight of blood, sexual arousal, the "rush" of gambling, or the "high" of illegal substances to feel alive.

27

FINDING THE COURAGE TO SAY THIS ISN'T WORKING

This is certainly a necessary part of the cycle to address since the endpoint of upsetting consequences fuels self-loathing and vulnerability. This, in turn, justifies your decision to continue hurting yourself. You may have started reading this book or come in to treatment completely invested in your behavior, buying into the idea that this was the only realistic "lifejacket" available to you. As a result, you may be initially hesitant about owning up to the common negative outcomes that these behaviors create. Examining or talking about these outcomes does not mean you are agreeing to give up the behaviors *before you are ready to do so.* Hopefully, this reassurance will give you the strength you need to look at this part of the equation.

When you can find the courage to put aside your fears and defenses, and admit to the "down side" of your behaviors, you might tap into intense issues. You need and deserve a safe environment in order to identify the universal feelings of shame, guilt, or disappointment in yourself. You may also need to explore anger at your "lack of discipline," anxiety about your helplessness or fear about disapproval from others. Additional feelings might include discouragement about the "loss of control," and your overwhelming feelings of inadequacy and failure. It might help to refer back to the questionnaire you filled out in the very beginning of the workbook to re-visit the negative consequences you identified. Exploring these issues is a balancing act. You have to continue to hold out hope even as you face the painful reality about the toll your behavior has been taking. Here again is the value of letting a compassionate, trained professional help you with this part of the journey.

Changing your thought patterns is essential at this part of the cycle. Identifying negative outcomes is not meant to be shaming or discouraging. Rather, it is an opportunity to see the behavior from a more authentic and self-loving point of view. This might be your first chance to even consider the possibility that what you are doing is creating more harm than good. It shines a spotlight on the fact that self-harm is, by definition, re-victimizing, and begins to challenge long-held beliefs that it is a necessary way to re-claim power and control. In your most honest moments, you can begin to acknowledge that everything about the behavior is, in fact, incredibly disempowering and out of control.

When the timing feels right a powerful intervention can occur at this place in the cycle. Consider the possibility that engaging in behaviors that promote abuse and neglect of the body is a way for you to say, "My perpetrator was *right*. I am worthless and my body doesn't deserve to be nurtured or protected." Ideally, you will not want to accept the notion that your perpetrator was right. You won't like the idea that your present day choices both support and keep re-enacting the abusive ways in which you were treated in the past. This can be a breakthrough in treatment.

Even if you don't relate strongly to this idea at first, this is another good opportunity to think about a loved one from the past who knows your perpetrators were wrong and believes that your body didn't deserve to be harmed. When you look at this through the eyes of someone else you might be able to be more honest about the downside to your behaviors. One very helpful strategy is to write a letter to yourself, from the person who loves and cares about you, identifying the negative effects of your self-destructive acts. Writing it from the point of view of a supportive person tends to remove the shame.

Fifteen-year-old Valerie was able to write herself a moving letter imagining it was from her beloved, deceased grandmother. The letter shows remarkable insight and has none of the shame or blame Valerie usually feels when she talks about her sexual acting out.

Dear Valerie,

I feel so sad when I think about you having sex with boys you barely know. I understand this is a way for you to feel loved, and I wish I were still in your life so I could safely give you the love and attention you really need and deserve. These boys don't really care about you, and probably forget about you right after you sleep with them. The problem is that *you* don't forget, and it leaves you feeling ashamed, dirty, and even more alone. No matter how many boys you sleep with, it won't help you feel better about yourself, and the short-term satisfaction that you get when someone agrees to be with you, turns pretty quickly to bad feelings—so really, it's not worth it. I love you.

Love, Granny

WRITING EXERCISE: A SUPPORTIVE LETTER TO YOURSELF FROM A "LOVED ONE"

Take some time to think about a person or pet in your present or past. Let it be someone who truly cares about you and your wellbeing. If you can't think of anyone at this time, you can use a loving, nurturing person from a book, film, or TV program. Imagine that they are writing you a letter, telling you in a compassionate way that your behaviors are harmful or victimizing. Write about how they would lovingly encourage you to replace those behaviors with healthier ones.

_____

_____

_____

_____

_____

_____

_____

_____

_____

_____

_____

_____

_____

_____

_____

_____

_____

_____

When you are ready, here's a chance to write a second letter, perhaps from someone else.

_____

_____

_____

_____

_____

_____

_____

_____

_____

_____

_____

_____

_____

_____

_____

_____

_____

_____

_____

_____

_____

Just as you found the courage to identify and access the part of you that engages in acts of self-harm, it is equally important and healing to access the most loving and wisest part of you that understands, deep down, how troubling these behaviors are for you. I know this part lives inside of you. It may even have been the part of you that bought this workbook, and has enabled you to stay focused and honest as you worked on all of the challenging journaling and drawing assignments! Maybe you accessed this part when you considered giving up on the work, yet found yourself returning to it, letting yourself move forward in your healing journey. Perhaps this is the part that brings you back to your therapist's office each week, or has become open to the idea of getting outside support at some time in the future. A wise and loving part can encourage you to take the appropriate medication, walk away from an unsafe situation, use your voice to advocate for your needs and rights, put down an instrument of self-harm and try CARESS.

The more you can describe and understand this part of yourself, the more easily you will be able to draw upon it for comfort, guidance, wisdom, and support. Using the same strategies you tried when identifying the self-destructive part, take some time to fully acknowledge, honor, and own this wonderful part of you. Keep in mind that this part is totally non-judgmental, mature, creative, kind, loving, patient, and nurturing. And it feels all of those things towards *you*, not just other people. If other thoughts or feelings find their way into this exercise, it means you have strayed away from the wisest part. Stop, breathe, and then try again to re-connect with your wisdom.

WRITING AND DRAWING EXERCISE: IDENTIFYING THE WISEST PART OF YOU

1) I will be describing the most compassionate and loving part of me. This part of me feels _____ years old.

2) When I visualize this part of me I see:

_____

_____

_____

_____

_____

_____

_____

_____

_____

_____

_____

_____

_____

_____

_____

3) Draw the part that holds your wisest thoughts and most loving feelings:

4) The adjectives I could use to describe the part that has self-love and care might be:

_____   _____

_____   _____

_____   _____

_____   _____

_____   _____

5) The sensations I feel in my body when I access this part of me include:

_____   _____

_____   _____

_____   _____

_____   _____

_____   _____

6) The colors, shapes and lines that illustrate those sensations might be:

7) The emotions I feel when I access this part of me include:

_____   _____

_____   _____

_____   _____

_____   _____

_____   _____

8) The colors, shapes, and lines that might express those emotions are:

9) I can have compassion for this part of me because:

_____

_____

_____

_____

_____

_____

_____

WRITING EXERCISE: A LETTER FROM THE WISEST PART OF YOU

When you are ready, here is an opportunity to write a letter to yourself, from the MOST LOVING PART OF YOU! The part that understands why your self-destructive behaviors are unfair to you, and a part that truly knows and believes that you no longer need those behaviors in your life. You don't need to write this all at one time. Just add to it as your insights grow!

_____

_____

_____

_____

_____

_____

_____

_____

_____

_____

_____

_____

_____

_____

_____

_____

_____

_____

_____

_____

_____

_____

Since you may be vulnerable to automatically putting yourself down, another meaningful intervention is to re-frame a relapse or setback as an opportunity to learn and grow. When you feel safe enough to think about and talk about your relapses you can use them as "teaching moments." It becomes an opportunity to re-visit triggers and re-wind the tape. This lets you brainstorm about the "tipping points" and to think about what you could do differently the next time you're confronted with a similar situation. It helps to identify even the smallest successes in breaking the cycle. This might be when you thought about doing CARESS, acted out for a shorter period of time, re-grounded more quickly, or didn't hurt yourself as severely as you have in the past.

Lastly, try to reassure yourself that the people who are close to you are not disappointed in you. They may initially react with anger or frustration when you relapse, but that is because they love you and are afraid your wellbeing and safety are compromised. You might ask those people in your life to express loving concern, along with the hope that you can still get better, rather than reacting with judgment or anger. If your friends and family are too scared to react appropriately, try telling yourself that their responses are rooted in love and do your best to dismiss their anger. If you have family that is just too mean or negative to give you the support you deserve, recognize that *they* are the problem and not you!

Although it is true that part of your healing will come from the experience of seeing loved ones hang in there with patience, empathy, and compassion, even when the people around you don't come through appropriately, the real power rests in how you talk to yourself about your relapses, not how others talk about it.

Keep in mind that a good therapist certainly should never "fire" you for doing your self-destructive behaviors, and should never give up on your capacity to grow and change. Given what you may have experienced with authority or parental figures in the past, you might assume your actions will create the same disapproving, distancing, or angry responses you got from your primary caretakers. Healthy, well-trained clinicians will not respond in those ways.

WRITING EXERCISE: RE-THINKING THE MESSAGES YOU GET FROM OTHERS ABOUT RELAPSES

Take a few minutes and think about the people in your life who are likely to weigh in about your relapses. In the blanks below, fill in the more common reactions they might have, whether those responses are positive or negative. Then give yourself the opportunity to re-think where those reactions come from, and what they are really trying to communicate, but might not know how.

1) Identify a person in your life who reacts to your relapses:

_____

_____

What they might typically say:

_____

_____

_____

_____

What they might typically do:

_____

_____

_____

_____

Where their reaction might be coming from:

_____

_____

_____

_____

What they might ACTUALLY be thinking or feeling:

_____

_____

_____

_____

2) Identify a person in your life who reacts to your relapses:

_____

_____

What they might typically say:

_____

_____

_____

_____

What they might typically do:

_____

_____

_____

_____

Where their reaction might be coming from:

_____

_____

_____

_____

What they might ACTUALLY be thinking or feeling:

_____

_____

_____

_____

WRITING EXERCISE: RE-THINKING YOUR OWN MESSAGES ABOUT RELAPSES

1) What I might typically say to myself or others:

_____

_____

What I might typically do:

_____

_____

_____

_____

_____

_____

Where my reaction might be coming from:

_____

_____

_____

_____

_____

_____

What I might ACTUALLY be thinking or feeling:

_____

_____

_____

_____

_____

_____

2) What I might typically say to myself or others:

_____

_____

What I might typically do:

_____

_____

_____

_____

_____

_____

Where my reaction might be coming from:

_____

_____

_____

_____

_____

_____

What I might ACTUALLY be thinking or feeling:

_____

_____

_____

_____

_____

_____

28

BEING COMPASSIONATE WHEN YOU ARE FEELING VULNERABLE

As you continue to work from your "personalized" cycle of self-harm take the time to process your areas of vulnerability. A great way to connect with this is to go back to the body. Notice what happens in your body as you sit with the negative outcomes. Does your body become rigid, tense, constricted, collapsed? You can more easily access your vulnerable states by noticing what your body is "saying" through gaze, posture, muscle tone, and breathing. Sometimes the body holds vulnerability in very specific places. Many people feel tightness in their chest or stomach, a lump in their throat, a clenching of the jaw, thighs, or fists. Breathing can become quick and shallow, while shoulders slump forward and eye contact is broken. These are all potential ways for your body to say, "I feel unsafe, embarrassed, defeated, frightened, and vulnerable."

At this phase of the cycle, you will benefit from learning how to be more assertive and to use appropriate behaviors for self-protection. You can reduce your vulnerability in the world by practicing how to make and sustain eye contact, along with having more awareness of your posture, stance, and tone of voice. If you are working with a therapist, role playing more assertive verbal and non-verbal responses to potentially triggering situations and intimidating people will help you slowly gain mastery over your learned response of remaining passive.

You may need outside support to help you understand the difference between "assertive" and "aggressive" responses. When you assert yourself, you are able to ask for what you need while staying sensitive to other peoples' feelings. When you are aggressive, you ask for what you want without taking into consideration the needs and feelings of others. If your perpetrators modeled aggressive behaviors then being assertive may be a new concept for you. Growing up with trauma and dysfunction, you are only shown two ways to be in the world: passive (victim) or aggressive (perpetrator). Once you figure out that you don't want to be a victim anymore you may initially swing to the other extreme and be too aggressive. Working on this issue in therapy helps you find your way back to the middle ground, where you can practice being assertive without feeling like a perpetrator.

Another effective strategy to address emotional or physical vulnerability is a guided imagery technique that invites you to visualize a protective shield of colorful light that surrounds and protects you. You can also tune in to the warmth or coolness of this light and color. You are powerful, assertive, and safe when you are bathed in this light. Go back to the body and tap into the sensations associated with this newfound sense of safety. Pair those positive sensations with a thought that strengthens the idea of being safe and strong. With practice, this becomes an inner resource that can quickly be called upon when you suddenly find yourself in vulnerable situations, or when you know, in advance, that you will be confronted by something or someone triggering.

> Throughout his childhood, 16-year-old Edward had to deal with a lot of teasing and inappropriately physically aggressive behaviors from his older brother. He grew up sharing a bedroom, so the taunts and painful "wrestling matches" were constant. Edward confessed that he never felt his parents protected him enough. Since his brother was too scary to confront, Edward had been communicating and trying to process his rage through self-mutilating behaviors. When his brother went off to college the self-harm dramatically decreased. However, his brother was coming home for Spring break, and Edward worried that he would start cutting again, so he wanted a way to feel "safer" and less vulnerable with his brother. One of the resources he used was visualizing a "bronze shield of warm light," that gave him a sense of "strength and power." He imagined his brother standing near him, and made the image stronger, memorizing the confident sensations he felt in his legs and on his chest and arms. We deepened the experience by pairing the feelings with thoughts that promoted self-protection and self-worth. As a result, he had a more powerful sense of himself and reported that his brother "left him alone" when he came home.

Visualization Exercise: Protection of Light and Color

Take the time to practice this strategy, choosing a soothing color to use as a source of protection. Experiment with intensifying or changing the color and see if you can add either a feeling of warmth or coolness to the color as a way of deepening the experience.

Feelings of vulnerability can also be reduced when you focus on strategies that help you set better limits with others. This often takes the form of learning how to say "No" in a way that is convincing and believable. The more a verbal "No" matches your body language, the less taken advantage of you will feel. Saying "No" with a strong voice, while standing tall and maintaining eye contact is a much more credible "No" than one that is said looking down with slumped posture in a small, wavering voice. This does take practice, as the experiences from childhood, cultural messages, or an abusive intimate relationship may have reinforced the idea that it is disrespectful, unsafe, or wrong to say "No" in such an assertive way.

Behavioral Exercise: Saying "No" Assertively

When you have private time, stand in front of a full-length mirror and practice saying "No." Pay attention to your posture, eye contact, and tone of voice. Notice the difference between saying "No" assertively, versus saying "No" in an unconvincing, passive way. If you have difficulty being assertive, use this exercise as another opportunity to re-connect with that wise, self-loving part and try tapping into the assertive body language and tone of voice that comes from that part.

In addition, you may need to re-define the boundaries, or the invisible lines that define separateness or closeness between people, in many of your personal and professional relationships in order to feel less vulnerable in the world. This may initially feel difficult and produce guilt. You may need the support and permission of a trusted friend, family member, or therapist in order to hold those newly formed boundaries. You may also need guidance in working through any fear or anxiety that comes up when you imagine how others will receive these new boundaries. It helps to first identify current boundaries in relationships and then allow yourself to redefine them if they interfere with your right to safety or privacy, place unreasonable or unrealistic expectations on you, or leave you feeling too vulnerable.

WRITING EXERCISE: IDENTIFYING AND RE-THINKING BOUNDARIES IN SIGNIFICANT RELATIONSHIPS

Fill in the following statements to explore this issue of boundaries in your current relationships. When you are finished be sure to soothe or calm yourself.

A1) Identify an important relationship in your life that leaves you feeling vulnerable:

_____

_____

2) Describe the current boundaries and the way in which you do/don't set limits with this person:

_____

_____

_____

_____

_____

_____

3) Identify what you could do to shift the boundaries so you feel more assertive and less vulnerable:

_____

_____

_____

_____

_____

_____

4) Describe what you think and feel when you consider shifting the boundaries in the ways you've identified above:

_____

_____

_____

_____

_____

B1) Identify an important relationship in your life that leaves you feeling vulnerable:

_____

_____

2) Describe the current boundaries and the way in which you do/don't set limits with this person:

_____

_____

_____

_____

_____

_____

_____

3) Identify what you could do to shift the boundaries so you feel more assertive and less vulnerable:

_____

_____

_____

_____

_____

_____

_____

_____

4) Describe what you think and feel when you consider shifting the boundaries in the ways you've identified above:

_____

_____

_____

_____

_____

_____

_____

C1) Identify an important relationship in your life that leaves you feeling vulnerable:

_____

_____

2) Describe the current boundaries and the way in which you do/don't set limits with this person:

_____

_____

_____

_____

_____

3) Identify what you could do to shift the boundaries so you feel more assertive and less vulnerable:

_____

_____

_____

_____

4) Describe what you think and feel when you consider shifting the boundaries in the ways you've identified above:

_____

_____

_____

_____

Lastly, you benefit greatly when you seek out and strengthen your external network of support. Normalizing your need and right to attach and connect with others helps to repair earlier losses and reduces the feeling of being alone in the world. At its core, emotional vulnerability is rooted in not feeling tethered to anything, and self-destructive acts keep alive this sense of isolation. As you grow in your efforts to re-connect you will heal basic attachment needs and discover newfound resources for comfort and self-soothing. In time, this makes self-destructive behaviors unnecessary and that becomes the first step in letting them go. You might want a therapist or trusted friend to help you explore and define the qualities that exist in loving, safe relationships, so you begin to gain an understanding of what to look for and what you deserve to have in your connections with other people.

DRAWING OR COLLAGING EXERCISE: CREATING AN IMAGE FOR CONNECTION AND ATTACHMENT

To strengthen this idea of reaching out to others for comfort and support, draw or collage images that reinforce this important idea of connecting and attaching to safe people in your life. What would that look like to you?

29

ON YOUR ROAD TO RECOVERY

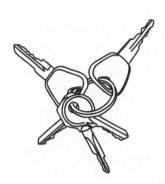

If you have reached this point in the workbook you have shown remarkable courage and strength! Hopefully, you have gained many insights along the way. The good news is, there is still so much to learn and so many ways for you to grow. Yes, this is good news! Your healing is a process and as long as you are growing, you are alive. Remember that a large part of your healing will come from sharing your thoughts and feelings with trusted people in your life. Let them bear witness, provide validation, compassion, and support. Allow them to comfort you through your grief and rejoice with you as you celebrate your successes. This will help you let go of secret keeping and shame, as well as the mistaken belief that you have to handle the difficulties of life alone.

There is no expectation that you won't falter at times. Try not to put that pressure on yourself. Taking steps forward and then a step or two back is a natural and inevitable part of the process. What matters is what you do with temporary setbacks. You could beat yourself up and use it as an excuse to stay stuck, or you can use relapses and feelings of fear or anxiety to motivate you and move you forward again. Every step you take becomes an opportunity to deepen your self-awareness, re-evaluate your actions, reach out for additional help, get another perspective, and learn something new.

One of the major themes of this workbook is holding on to the belief that you have power and you have choice. You can choose to communicate and self-soothe in ways that are destructive or in ways that are truly effective and healing. This is yours to choose and it will always be your choice. However, you owe it to yourself to make that choice from a place of self-love, self-awareness, empowerment, and an understanding of your current reality paired with a sense of hope for the future. Many times, choices are made from a "victim mentality" and a dysfunctional and distorted childhood tape that is frozen in time or rooted in untrue messages from perpetrators. As you disentangle your thoughts, feelings, and behaviors from the past, give yourself permission to re-assess and re-evaluate what you need, feel, and deserve. And then make choices from that newfound place.

Ironically, your struggle with self-destructive behaviors indicates you are resilient, creative, and driven to survive. Let go of any label that offers a "disease-based" explanation for your actions. That mindset won't help you move ahead with your life. You have been working so hard to manage your pain, share your experiences, short-circuit upsetting thoughts and feelings, and self-soothe. That means that somewhere inside of you is the will and desire to heal, live a more meaningful life, and connect with others. Wanting those things comes from the best part of you. And that part is your wisest and most loving self. You deserve guidance and support in learning how to accomplish those things in healthier, more gratifying, and positive ways.

At the same time, the parts of you that have tried to protect you from pain, or cling to past memories of pain, need to be comforted and reassured. When the wisest part of you can show empathy and compassion for your self-destructive and traumatized parts you are truly on the road to recovery.

The work you have done in this book, and continue to do as you re-visit the chapters and exercises at a future time, can help get you there. You have so much to be proud of, and it's important to let yourself feel proud! Remember, you have what it takes to take care of yourself and to heal. It's inside of you. And it's in your willingness to access and embrace the love and support of safe and trustworthy people in your life. You deserve this. Don't settle for anything less!

GLOSSARY OF TERMS

Analgesia—Not having any sensation of pain on the body. Often related to a dissociative or "zoned out" state.

Anorexia—An eating disorder characterized by the deliberate restriction of calories and intake of food. There is either a fear of becoming fat or the distorted belief that one is already overweight.

Anticipatory anxiety—Feeling worried about the possibility of becoming anxious in a future situation or interaction, especially if you felt anxious in that situation before.

Augmentation—Using a second prescribed medication to boost the effect of an anti-depressant.

Bingeing—An eating disorder characterized by secretly consuming large quantities and calories of food within a short period of time. The behavior usually continues until there is physical pain or exhaustion.

Body betrayal—Experiencing unwanted or confusing physical changes during adolescence. Although these changes are a normal part of development, they usually leave the teenager feeling embarrassed or not in control of their body.

Boundaries—The invisible lines people draw between themselves that indicate either a closeness or distance from one another.

CARESS—A strategy to use when confronted with the impulse to engage in a self-destructive behavior. Allows you to Communicate Alternatively, Release Endorphins, and Self-Soothe.

Childhood propaganda—The inaccurate, negative messages that perpetrators tell their victims. These messages have a profound impact on self-esteem, and create self-blame and shame.

Containment—Using visualization, writing, or drawing to create a safe way to set aside the things that might feel emotionally overwhelming until a person is ready to re-visit them.

De-coding—Interpreting the deeper, often unconscious, meaning of self-destructive behaviors.

De-pathologizing—A treatment concept that eliminates the idea of someone being "mentally ill" or "weak" as an explanation for their behavior.

De-personalization—Feeling like what is happening is not happening to your body. Often associated with the freeze response when experiencing trauma.

De-realization—Feeling like what is happening is a dream. Often associated with the freeze response when experiencing trauma.

Disengaged boundaries—A relationship where there is a lack of connection, attachment, or closeness between two people. This often leads to neglect or the absence of a caretaking figure.

Disorganized attachment—A dynamic in the parent–child relationship where the parent's behaviors are sometimes scary or abusive, and at other times the parent seems frightened by the child's needs and feelings.

Dissociation—"Spacing out" or "zoning out" as a way to mentally escape a threatening situation that cannot be physically escaped.

Emotional incest—A dynamic in the parent–child relationship that exists when a parent inappropriately makes their child their confidante or "buddy," typically resulting in uncomfortable boundaries and confused feelings for the child. This often occurs when the other adult partner is unavailable to their spouse.

Endorphins—Naturally occurring opiates released by the brain to counter-act pain or trauma inflicted on the body.

Enmeshed boundaries—A situation where there is no real sense of "separateness" between two people. This leaves at least one person feeling suffocated, smothered, lacking in privacy, or violated by the other person.

Escape clause—Pre-planning ways to get out of a situation that might be triggering. This might include having a friend text you at a specific time when you are interacting with an intimidating person, so you have a built-in excuse to step away or leave.

Event marker—Doing something self-destructive on your body during a specific date or time, to unconsciously validate and remember an unspeakable abuse experience from the past.

Exercise bulimia—A form of purging that combines excessive exercise with a lack of sufficient calories.

External safety—Feeling secure in the world because your environment is soothing and safe, or you have comforting interactions with others.

Fight/flight response—A biologically hard-wired survival response when you are threatened. In an effort to feel safe, the body reacts by either aggressively fighting back, or by physically escaping a threatening situation.

Flashback—Re-living something traumatic from the past as if it were happening in the present moment. This is usually experienced through visual images, distressing thoughts, upsetting emotions, or body sensations.

Flooded—The feeling of being emotionally overwhelmed and unable to handle difficult experiences.

Freeze response—A biologically hard-wired survival response associated with dissociation. Usually manifests by holding still, not breathing, pretending to be asleep, physically collapsing, staying silent, or "submitting" in order to stay safe to get through a traumatic event.

Frozen in time thinking—Placing past experiences onto the present as if they are happening now. This usually manifests in people who were victimized in the past and still believe they are helpless in the present.

Hyper-vigilant—Staying extremely aware of and focused on one's environment and the actions of other people in order to feel safe in the world.

Internal safety—Feelings of being calm and secure that come from either soothing visual images in the mind, or relaxed body sensations.

Intervention sites—Different parts of the cycle of self-destructive behavior that provide opportunities to try something new and do something healthy when triggered.

Learned helplessness—A "normal" and familiar feeling of having no power or control. Usually the consequence of repeated past experiences where power and control was taken away.

Limbic system—The "smoke alarm" part of the brain that responds to sensory experiences and lets us know when there is danger or threat. This part of the brain connects to the fight/flight/freeze response. It is never capable of insight.

Loving resource—Using positive memories and feelings from a meaningful and safe relationship as a resource for comfort, even when that person is not actually present.

Meta-communication—Expressing thoughts and feelings through our faces, tone of voice, body language, or behaviors rather than through words.

Non-protective bystanders—Caretakers who do not directly inflict harm, yet still traumatize because they are unable or unwilling to shield or protect a victim from someone who is harmful or abusive.

Normalizing—A strengths-based approach that helps clients recognize that their thoughts, feelings, and behaviors are in keeping with the way other people think, feel, and behave.

Over-generalizing—The negative and distorted belief that if something upsetting or threatening happened once, it will keep happening to you.

Pacing—A conscious choice made by either the client or the therapist to do emotional or difficult therapy work slowly so it never feels overwhelming.

Pain narrative—Facts and information about something upsetting or traumatic that has been experienced in the past. Sometimes this is conscious and other times not in one's conscious memory.

Personalizing—Taking ownership of an experience and believing it has happened because of something you said or did. Holding yourself responsible for an event that is typically not your fault.

Pre-frontal cortex—The "thinking" and reasoning higher functioning part of the brain that helps us analyze, and think about cause and effect. This is the part of the brain that goes "off-line" when you are threatened.

PTSD—Post-Traumatic Stress Disorder. A diagnosis given to people who have experienced or witnessed an event that posed the threat of death or threatened one's physical, sexual, or psychological safety and integrity. The trauma may be re-experienced through flashbacks or nightmares, or there can be a numbing and avoidance of things that are associated with the traumatic event. This can also affect people who are first responders or who are repeatedly subjected to other people's traumatic experiences.

Purging—An eating disordered behavior where food is eliminated after it is eaten. This can be accomplished through self-imposed vomiting, enemas, or laxative abuse.

Re-enacting—Engaging in behaviors that unconsciously allow you to re-live a past traumatic experience so it can be revealed and others can bear witness to it.

Re-framing—Looking at an experience from a different, more positive perspective. This is usually done to introduce a concept of hope or to challenge a belief that is inaccurate.

Re-grounding—Engaging in a behavior that helps bring your awareness back to your body and the present moment. Especially useful when you start to dissociate or zone out.

Relapse—Resuming an addictive or self-destructive behavior after a period of abstinence.

Remission—Experiencing a complete alleviation of all symptoms of depression while taking medication. This leads to a full and complete return to good mental health.

Response—Feeling some symptom relief while taking medication for the treatment of depression, yet still having lingering depressive symptoms and not being completely cured.

Re-storying—Trying to change the outcome of a traumatic experience in order to re-claim a feeling of power, control, or closure.

Secure attachment—Raised by caretakers who are consistent, reliable, willing and able to bond, protect, and nurture.

Self-medicate—Using unhealthy behaviors that typically numb you, so deeper emotional pain isn't experienced.

Self-mutilation—Deliberately injuring, cutting, burning, or wounding the body to inflict pain, "feel better," become numb, or punish the body.

Sensory experiences—Things you see, hear, taste, touch, and smell in your environment.

Sexual abuse—Any experience where a child, adolescent, or adult feels an invasion of boundaries or privacy in regards to their body, or feels pressured, forced, or threatened to "participate" in or observe any sexual activity.

Sexual addiction—A diagnosis given to people who continue to engage in sexual activities despite the fact that their behavior causes problems in work, relationships, family, legal status, or health.

Sociopath—Someone who is completely lacking in a sense of empathy for others. As a result, they are capable of harming victims without any feeling of remorse, and may actually derive pleasure from inflicting pain on others.

Somatic experiences—Sensations you experience in your body, including tightness, tension, tingling, etc.

Standard safety contract—A signed agreement that states you will not engage in any unsafe behaviors. Typically used by mental health professionals who are trying to stop clients from doing self-destructive acts.

Strengths-based approach—A treatment perspective that focuses on what is "right" with a person rather than what is "wrong." This includes an acknowledgment of courage, resiliency, creativity, and the capacity to survive.

Subjective sense—Your take on reality, which may or may not be rooted in objective fact, but still influences your thoughts, feelings, or behaviors, and becomes your "truth."

Substance abuse—Excessive use of drugs and alcohol in ways that negatively affect your work performance, relationships, legal status, school performance, or health.

Survivor guilt—Feeling upset about having endured and gotten through a threatening situation, while others may have gotten hurt. This can manifest by feeling that you should have somehow protected or saved the other person, or stopped their abuse from happening.

Trauma—Any experience that causes a fundamental threat to one's physical, emotional, sexual, or psychological safety and wellbeing. Usually creates feelings of helplessness, fear, shame, terror, anger, and loss. Is often managed by going into a fight/flight or freeze response in order to survive.

Trichotillomania—A form of self-harm that involves pulling out your eyelashes, eyebrows, beard hair, hair on the head, or pubic hair, for the purposes of self-soothing or numbing.

Triggers—Experiences, often relating to the five senses, that remind you of painful things from the past. They cause an upset reaction in you, and leave you feeling as if the past is being relived in the present.

Tunnel vision—Having a limited, often negative view of yourself, what has happened to you, and your coping strategies.

Universalizing—A treatment approach that lets clients know they are not alone in their experiences, thoughts, feelings, and behaviors.

INDEX